Acclaim for Bob Rich's
From Depression to Contentment

"Have you been diagnosed with depression? Do you believe you're stuck with it, because of your genetics, your brain chemistry, your past or your circumstances? Luckily, you're not. In *From Depression to Contentment*, Dr. Bob Rich reveals how you can re-engineer your life to beat depression. The book is empowering, empathetic and written with great intelligence. The guide draws on many proven therapeutic techniques, and Dr. Bob adds something new and creative to each one, making them even more powerful. The author generously interweaves his own story of recovering from depression with other case studies and examples, making the book very relatable and easy to understand. The essential message of the book is that you can beat depression by improving the quality of your thinking, your behavior and your life. There are a couple of sections that appear to veer away from the main topic, but don't skip them, because they offer uplifting stories full of hope, inspiration and motivation. Overall, a wonderfully refreshing and practical self-help guide to healing from depression and living a fulfilling life."

Beth Burgess, psychotherapist, author of
Instant Wisdom, The Happy Addict, and *The Recovery Formula*

"Depression can be turned into a positive and can actually enrich our lives if we just try. It is not easy to acquire the skills and the knowledge necessary to learn to cope well and to recover, but this book will make the effort easier. Specific interventions - like guided imagery and mindfulness meditation - are suggested and explained. All-in-all, this is a valuable manual on how to live well with depression and acquire the right skills and knowledge that will tame the depression to a point where the person will live well without being affected by symptoms."

Alfredo Zotti, author of
Alfredo's Journey: An Artist's Creative Life with Bipolar Disorder

"If you're depressed and need someone who 'gets' you, who's been there, and who can walk you through the journey toward living a life worth living, then *From Depression to Contentment* will be your new best friend. Bob's a straight shooter who tells it as it is. He meets you where you are and can lead you home to yourself."

Petrea King, CEO and Founder of Quest for Life Foundation

"Combining his personal and professional experience, Dr. Rich offers a valuable self-help tool for those seeking additional insight for coping with depression. The suggested exercises are easy to follow with an explanation of what they are helping with. And he does it all with a great sense of humor woven in."

Chynna T. Laird, author of *Not Just Spirited: A Mom's Sensational Journey with Sensory Processing Disorder (SPD)*

"Dr. Bob Rich has created a simple and direct guide to beat back depression for good. Put forth in easy to digest bits, the approach uses small, effective steps to move past the overwhelm of depression. Written in a conversational tone, Dr. Rich expresses his personal and professional understanding of the toll depression takes on one's life, while avoiding technicalities of the condition. If you're looking to move past depression without drugs, then this practical guidebook is for you."

Diane Wing, M.A., author of
The Happiness Perspective: Seeing *Your Life Differently*

"This book lives up to its title: it is a course in and of self-therapy, starting with first aid tips and ending with a "meaning of life" positivity-oriented approach, akin to logotherapy. It effectively surveys the literature about depression and debunks psychiatry's money-fueled pretensions to be a science. Instead, it offers a down-to-earth classifica-tion of various types of sadness: from dysthymia to Bipolar Disorder and two dozen other types of malaise in between. The book assigns useful homework as a coping strategy for each variant of depression."

Sam Vaknin, Ph.D. author of
Malignant Self-love: Narcissism Revisited

From Depression to Contentment

A Self-Therapy Guide

Bob Rich, Ph.D.

Loving Healing Press

Ann Arbor, MI

Learn more at http://anxietyanddepression-help.com

ISBN-13: 978-1-61599-435-9 paperback
ISBN-13: 978-1-61599-436-6 hardcover
ISBN-13: 978-1-61599-437-3 eBook

Library of Congress Cataloging-in-Publication Data

Names: Rich, Robert, 1943- author.
Title: From depression to contentment : a self-therapy guide / Bob Rich, Ph.D.
Description: Ann Arbor, MI : Loving Healing Press, [2019] | Includes
   bibliographical references and index.
Identifiers: LCCN 2019000127| ISBN 9781615994359 (pbk. : alk. paper) | ISBN
   9781615994366 (hardcover : alk. paper) | ISBN 9781615994373 (ebook)
Subjects: LCSH: Depression, Mental--Treatment. | Depression, Mental--Popular
   works.
Classification: LCC RC537 .R523 2019 | DDC 616.85/27--dc23
LC record available at https://lccn.loc.gov/2019000127

Published by
Loving Healing Press
5145 Pontiac Trail
Ann Arbor, MI 48105

www.LHPress.com
info@LHPress.com

Tollfree: 888-761-6268 (USA/CAN)
Fax: 734-663-6861

Contents

Chapter 1: You have to be crazy to stay sane in a crazy world ... 1
This is a User's Guide 2

Chapter 2: Basic First Aid 5
Whatever Your Depression Tells You, Do the Opposite 5
Healthy Eating 7
Satisfying Sleep 8
Regular Physical Exercise 10
Regular Fun 11
Creativity 11
Social Connectedness 12
Meaning 14

Chapter 3: Relaxation and Meditation 19
Muscular Relaxation 19
Mindfulness Meditation 22
Guided Imagery 26

Chapter 4: Know Your Enemy 31
The Conventional View 31
Sources of Sadness 33
The Causes of Human Suffering 37
The Development of Resilience 50

Chapter 5: Controlling Depression 53
Fixing the thinking 54
Rewriting your story 68
Act The Way You Want To Be 72

Chapter 6: The Cure for Depression 79
The Destination 79
Don't Like Your World? Change it 84
Processing Trauma 86
Loving the Inner Monster 89
You Get What You Send 91

The Resilient Mindset 93

Moving Hedonic Adaptation 96

Flow 104

Chapter 7: Spiritual Care 107

My Greatest Teacher 107

Reincarnation 109

Equanimity 122

Chapter 8: Depression in the Family 127

Caring for the Carer 128

Inducing change and growth 130

Chapter 9: Dealing with Relapse 135

References 137

About the Author 142

Index 143

Important Notes for the Reader

- If you are feeling suicidal, contact telephone help services that are available almost everywhere. In the USA, call 1-800-273-8255, in the UK 1850 60 90 90.

- If you want to discontinue antidepressant medication, you must do so slowly and gradually, under medical supervision.

- This is not a book to simply read, but a *handbook* for changing your life. There are homework tasks in many places. Some of them will need weeks, or even months, to implement. Take them seriously, and you'll have done very powerful self-therapy that has a good chance of improving your very world, and yourself within it.

- I suggest one of three ways of doing this program: 1. A quick read through, then a step-by-step progress, probably taking months; 2. A quick read, then focusing on the chapters you need most at this time; or 3. Front-to-end progression, carrying out all the tasks.

- Links to web pages are scattered throughout. Since clicking them in some versions (e.g., paperback) is not particularly effective, I've listed them all, as well as all the homework tasks, at http://bobswriting.com/dlinks.html. If you have a PDF edition, note that the cursor will change to a "pointer" when you hover over a link to remind you that this is indeed a clickable item.

- Something works for everyone, but nothing works for everyone. If you find that the program in this book doesn't work for you, the best investment you can make is 8 to 20 sessions of therapy with a good psychologist.

You need to be crazy to stay sane in a crazy world

Pessimism vs. optimism is one of the dimensions of human personality. Interesting research shows that pessimists are consistently more realistic than optimists. This is because reality is far worse than you could think without getting depressed.

Diagnosed depression is a galloping epidemic. The facts are admirably summarized by Tyrell and Elliot (https://tinyurl.com/bobrich01). Their main conclusions are worth repeating:

- Major depression is the No. 1 psychological disorder in the western world. It is growing in all age groups, in virtually every community, and the growth is seen most in the young, especially teens. At the rate of increase, it will be the second most disabling condition in the world by 2020, behind heart disease.

- More than ever, we need to look at alternatives to drugs that will equip us to deal effectively with the triggers that allow depression to take hold again and again. This is where drug treatments fail.

- People of all ages, backgrounds, lifestyles, and nationalities suffer from major depression, with a few exceptions.

- Up to 20% of people experience symptoms of depression.

According to Martin Seligman, depression in 1984 was 10 times as frequent as in the 1950s.

So, if you're depressed, it's not the fault of your biology, individual circumstances, or personality, but of the world you live in. Maybe you're just smarter and more perceptive than others who are lucky enough to carry on OK in a toxic culture.

If depression was mainly a matter of heredity, it wouldn't be a growing problem. The fact of its rapid increase points the finger at society, not the individual. Nevertheless, the causation of any psychological reaction is always complex. To learn to gain a less painful way of reacting, we need to understand what leads us to extended periods of sadness. So, read on!

This is a User's Guide

Depression is a way of seeing the world; a way of being. It isn't a disease, a disorder, or a chemical imbalance. It's not something you are, or have, but something you DO.

There is a lot of evidence for my statement, but this is a user's guide, not some academic treatise. I am not interested in getting into scholarly arguments.

The causes, nature and treatment of depression are best described in an excellent article Michael Gathercole published in the *Australian Journal of Counselling Psychology* in 2004. It didn't make the impact it should have, so I've reproduced it with permission on my website http://anxietyanddepression-help.com as "An important NEW MODEL OF DEPRESSION." And that's almost all the academic stuff you'll get from me in this book.

I have two credentials for writing this user's guide.

First and most important, I personally lived with depression from infancy. Without realizing it, I started to do therapy on myself when I was 21. By 23, I had it in control all by myself. A crash would come occasionally—then I fixed it. This went on for another 20 years. When I was 43, I noticed that the depression was gone. Previous invariable triggers failed to drag me down. (My personal journey is described in two of my books: *Anikó: The stranger who loved me* http://bobswriting.com/aniko.html, and *Ascending Spiral: Humanity's last chance* http://bobswriting.com/ascending.html).

If I could do it, you can do it.

I did have a relapse in 2011, as a reaction to a loss I hadn't thought would affect me. Using the tools I'd developed to cure myself, I returned to contentment in three weeks.

Second, I have a Ph.D. in psychology, and provided psychotherapy for decades. So, I do understand all the science, and know what I am talking about. If I could be successfully of service to my clients, I can be successfully of service to you.

As with any manual, you need to DO what it recommends. You can't learn tennis by reading a book about how to do it. You can't change your world by reading a book about how to do it.

I'll start with first aid, which helps everyone in any situation. Then we'll get an understanding of depression, and finally go onto the specifics of living a contented life, even if we are on the planet of the insane ("normal people" who do what everyone does).

2 Basic First Aid

There are seven requirements for a contented life. All of them may be present to varying degrees. If you have a good dose of all seven, you'll have the inner strength and resilience to support you in your fight against Depression, Anxiety and similar devils.

Your Depression knows this. It knows the list, even if you don't. It protects itself by sabotaging as many of these requirements as possible. It can do this very well. So, first aid, the way to fight back, is to return these seven features into your life. The rule is:

Whatever Your Depression Tells You, Do the Opposite

I'll briefly discuss the list here, so you can take immediate action, before examining what depression is and isn't, then presenting tools for controlling it, and finally tools for getting rid of it altogether—most of the time.

The seven first-aid measures are:

- Healthy eating
- Satisfying sleep
- Regular physical exercise
- Regular fun
- Creativity
- Social connectedness
- Meaning

Since this is a first aid list, I've ordered it so that the easiest to implement is at the top.

Note what is NOT on the list:

- Wealth

- Success
- Status
- Beauty
- Romantic love
- Youth
- Physical health
- Absence of pain
- Freedom from stress
- Having a job
- Getting out of your job/marriage/stressful social situation

...and all the other reasons people tend to associate with their mood.

The last requirement, *meaning*, comes from the work of Viktor Frankl. You just have to read his inspiring book, *Man's Search for Meaning*. The other six come from anthropological research on the lifestyles of hunter-gatherer people. You see, genetically, we are identical to our ancestors from up to perhaps 10,000 years ago. By analyzing the lives of modern hunter-gatherers, anthropologists have extracted the essentials of the lifestyle humans have evolved in, and that's the list I've given you.

Think of my recommendations as antidepressants. Only, these antidepressants have several huge advantages over nasty little pills:

- Many of them are free. Those that cost money have other benefits. These benefits are what you pay for; the anti-depressant aspect is free.

- They have no undesirable side-effects. In fact, most of them have very pleasant and desirable side-effects.

- Like prescription antidepressants, they're habit-forming, but since they feel nice and do you good, this is an advantage rather than a disadvantage.

- The only withdrawal effect is the risk that Depression (or whatever your monster is) may return.

Let's now look at each of the seven requirements for contentment, see how monsters like Depression sabotage them, and how you can protect yourself.

Healthy Eating

Depression starves some people. It tricks others into ill health and obesity by getting them to eat too much, and all the wrong kinds of food. Either way, its job is easy in today's crazy society: even people who are not suffering distress are likely to eat badly, and many of the common foods are full of stuff that does you harm.

Eating Too Little

Fred didn't want to get counseling. He knew it couldn't possibly help him—nothing could. Life was hopeless, and that was that. But when he mentioned killing himself to his doctor, he was given my leaflet and ordered to see me. He canceled the first appointment, because his car (conveniently) broke down. He didn't show up for the second. I phoned him, and after a long conversation, he at last made the effort to be there the third time.

Sound familiar? It may well be if you're in the grip of deep Depression.

When we finally sat face to face, I asked him what was making his life so miserable that he contemplated suicide. A whole list of woes emerged, but the top item was, "I can't eat. If I have something, I feel like chucking up."

"Have you ever done so?"

"No, but it sure feels like it."

I knew that his doctor had checked him out for any physical problems, so I told him, "Food is medicine. Eat a tiny bit, doesn't matter how it makes you feel, and do this every now and then until you have enough to keep you going."

We organized a few strategies. He bought grapes, and popped them one at a time, ten minutes or so apart. He made a cheese sandwich, cut it into eight pieces and ate one piece, went on with whatever he was doing, ate another little square, and so on.

At first, the nausea persisted. But, while he fed his body regardless of how bad he felt after it, he was starving his Depression. Within a couple of weeks, he could eat a normal meal.

By the way, Fred wasn't his real name, and I'm not even saying if the client was male or female. All my examples in this book are real, but I've changed identifying details. Where I could, I've asked the person's permission for inclusion.

Eating Too Much

Depression tricks you into becoming overweight through "comfort eating" or "boredom eating," and always the things you swore you won't touch (but have handy all the same). You feel guilty, and put on weight—and this gives something else that your Depression can use to beat you over the head.

First aid is to get rid of all the wrong foods and store up on things that are good for you: apples, carrots, celery, chewy dried apricots, and nuts of various kinds. When you feel like some comfort food, eat a small amount of one of these, then congratulate yourself. Tell all the people in your life that you're switching your food intake in this way, and ask them to help by keeping the problem foods away from you.

Shopping is the danger time. Make it a rule: you come with a shopping list. If it's not on the list, don't buy it. The internet allows you to be up to date on specials in your neighborhood store, so even a reduced price shouldn't lead to impulse buying. If you do slip and buy something from the old times, punish yourself by giving it away. Then, being generous to someone else will make you feel good about yourself.

Satisfying Sleep

As with food, Depression can trick you into either too much or too little. Or it can keep you awake all night, and then you'll feel sluggish and sleepy all day.

Too Little Sleep

Do you lie in bed, your mind going around and around, torturing you with thoughts you'd rather not have? Among them will be the thought, *I MUST get to sleep! I'll be so tired tomorrow! Oh, will I never get to sleep?* On and on the wicked merry-go-round goes, keeping you awake.

Some facts about the nature of sleep will help. Sleep has several stages, which can be grouped into two: rest, and dream time (called "rapid eye movement" or REM sleep, because when you dream, your eyes visibly move under your closed eyelids). You can't do without REM sleep. No matter how many hours you spend asleep, if someone wakes you the moment your eyes start moving, you'll be like the walking dead in the morning. If you put all your REM times together, they'll amount to about two hours. You're guaranteed to get that much during an average awful night of disturbed sleep. So, typically, lack of REM sleep isn't the problem. It is that you haven't rested at all during your stay in bed.

It actually makes no difference whether you're awake or asleep for the remainder of the time. As long as your body is relaxed, you'll be as rested as if you were asleep. In contrast, sleeping while tense doesn't rest you at all. You can sleep deeply for ten hours and wake tired, if during all that time your body was like a compressed spring.

So, the first aid trick is to learn muscular relaxation. I'll teach you in the next chapter, because it's an important tool in its own right.

Then, **it is just as restful to lie there, eyes closed, breathing softly, your body completely relaxed, as if you were asleep.**

As you breathe in, feel air going in your nose, into your chest, and your tummy rising. As you breathe out focus on tummy going down, air out of your chest, relatively warm air coming out of your nose.

It's good to fill your mind with a mantra: something you say over and over till it becomes boring, then till it becomes meaningless, and still do it. I use the mantra **just as... ...restful** to remind me of what I'm doing: resting whether I am awake or asleep. That means, you're concentrating on four things all the time.

The mantra is true. But even if it wasn't, it would cut through the negative thinking that's keeping you awake. Get relaxed. Lie there with your eyes closed, breathing softly, and keep saying this mantra to yourself. You'll soon be asleep. And even if for any reason you're still awake, you'll feel rested in the morning.

Too Much Sleep

Tony was a nice, decent 17-year-old. He and his group of close friends did everything together. Unfortunately, that involved substance abuse. One night, a member of the group murdered his best friend, while out of his mind on marijuana and alcohol. (In some people, marijuana can induce intense terror or rage.)

Tony held the dying boy during his last moments. Months later, he was required to testify against his friend in court. Not surprisingly, he needed counseling.

I asked him how he was affected. He told me that the worst thing was that he couldn't be bothered to do anything. He took "sickies" from work as an apprentice mechanic, because he couldn't get up in the morning, had no energy. All he wanted to do was sleep. "What's the point of doing anything anyway?"

He hadn't realized that he was in the grip of Depression, a natural aspect of grieving.

He agreed that whenever his grief tried to talk him out of doing something, he'd force himself to do just that. He set his alarm clock for the usual time he needed to rise for work, even on weekends and holidays.

"If you feel too bad to go to work, then maybe you need to stay at home, but still get up at the right time," I told him. "Then, do all the other preparatory things you do on an ordinary day: have a shower, shave, get dressed, eat breakfast. After that, if you want to, you can undress and return to bed."

When he did this, he ended up going to work (well, not on weekends and holidays). The first step is always the hardest.

On the days when he defied his grief, he actually felt good, in power, for having done so.

Regular Physical Exercise

Many people do things that get them tired, but that is not the kind of exercise I mean. You need to work up a sweat, and find yourself puffing for air. When you do this, your body generates chemicals called "endorphins." When endorphins settle in certain receptor sites, you feel good, happy, full of energy. So, aerobic exercise is a holiday from depression.

Have a skipping rope handy, or do a few star-jumps, or go for a brisk ten-minute walk, and you'll feel good for a while.

Exercise can be the wedge that allows you to escape the trap of Depression. It can become a "good addiction." If you do exactly the right amount of exercise for your current level of fitness, you'll enjoy the experience. So, you'll be motivated to do more.

There are three dangers: to overdo it, so exercising also develops negative reactions; to set yourself unrealistic goals, so Depression can then torture you with thoughts of failure and inadequacy; and to compare yourself with others.

This exercise is strictly an antidepressant. It doesn't matter whether you're improving or not. It doesn't matter if someone else can do it much better. All that matters is that you develop a tool for feeling good.

It may seem like a paradox, but keeping records is a great motivator. Without trying to improve, you will, and this'll be obvious when you check distances and speeds of walking, or the number of pushups you do, or the weight you use for a particular exercise, compared to what you could manage a few months ago.

Regular Fun

How can you have fun when you're miserable?

You often do. I did an experiment once. My friend Georgia and I went to a concert. She is a musician—and was suffering from severe depression. As I watched her, it was obvious that she thoroughly enjoyed herself. Her eyes never left the performers. I could see that she was up on stage with them. Her mouth was half open much of the time, her body subtly moved with the rhythm. After the performance, she chatted with me, bought a CD and talked for some time with the players, smiled at strangers.

I saw her again a few days later. "How did you enjoy the concert?" I asked.

"Oh... it was all right I suppose." Her tone of voice was bored, flat, shoulders were slumped forward, and she didn't look at me. She was in the pits, and couldn't even imagine that a few days previously she might have had fun.

That's what the doom-colored glasses of suffering do to you.

Don't believe your Depression when it tells you that you never have fun, can't have fun, there is no such thing as fun.

There have been times in your past when life was OK. If you're in the pits now, chances are you won't remember them. But try. Think back to times when you got on with your life, and the misery was absent. What did you do for fun then?

Whatever it was, deliberately schedule it into your week.

Creativity

One reason for the high incidence of suffering in technological society is that so many people stop doing creative things for months, even years at a time. They go on day after day, week after week, year after year, round and round the same treadmill of routine and boredom. Get up in the morning, commute to work, go through the motions, come home, veg out in front of the idiot box, go to bed... who wouldn't be depressed? And these are the lucky ones who have a job.

For many people, life is drab. Housework is a chore. Kids are an unending stream of problems. Work is a chunk out of your life. And when you go on holidays, you come back so exhausted you need to recover from them.

Introduce creative activities. Here are a few examples:

- Whatever your work, find ways of doing it with enthusiasm, seeking new ways, learning new skills, aiming for new achievements.

- Attend a course. This could be anything from learning the skills for a new hobby to a Ph.D. My first client was a lady who enrolled at University for a degree in Divinity. That's how I knew she no longer needed my services.

- Play music.

- Some people get a lot out of gardening.

- Cooking can be highly creative, even cooking for one person.

- Housework can be done creatively. Spend a couple of hours cleaning a room, then enjoy its welcoming feel.

- Outdoor activities like walking, cycling, fishing, nature observation can be highly creative if done in the right frame of mind.

- Then of course there are the activities usually thought of as creative: painting, making things with your hands, writing poetry or stories, composing music.

Where do you find the time for such things? Engaging in something like an item from this list gives you MORE time rather than less. This is because creativity recharges your inner batteries, and you'll be more efficient at everything you do.

Social Connectedness

Megan worked as a sales assistant in a huge department store. She described it as being a trained pair of hands and an automatic smile. To customers, she was a thing that took their money. She had no contact with other workers except during the lunch break, and even then, she knew they were not interested in her as a person. All the talk was on superficial topics she couldn't care less about. To her superiors, she knew herself to be no more than a number, someone to keep an eye on.

Irene worked in the same store. She loved her work, particularly the people aspect. She said some customers came regularly, and they always had a friendly chat with her. She'd watched their kids grow over the years. She took an interest in her colleagues, and several had become her friends, with frequent after-work contact.

Both these women came to me through the store's Employment Assistance program. Irene came for chronic pain management, because of a painful lower back, and Repetitive Stress Injury (RSI) in both wrists. It won't surprise you to find out that Megan came for help with Depression.

Research shows that a person needs to have close connections to other people. Being part of three (possibly overlapping) networks is the minimum, but more is better. I'm a loner, but when I learned about social connectedness, I counted mine. I was part of 20 networks.

Paul was the custodial parent of two daughters. His ex-wife had abused the girls, and he'd won sole custody, denying her access. He was also suicidally depressed. The only thing keeping him alive was that his death would impose terrible suffering on his daughters. When we worked together, the reason became clear: he only had ONE social network: he and his daughters. He had no feeling of connection to anyone else at all.

When you're in the grip of Depression, you want to avoid company. Also, others won't enjoy being with a grump. A third way Depression isolates you is by whispering that the people you care for are too good for you, and the best thing you can do is to separate from them.

Remember, whatever your Depression tells you, do the opposite. Remember, it's doom-colored glasses that hide the good things and focus on the bad.

It's important to note that I am not talking about introversion-extraversion here. People vary according to their need for being with others. The extreme extravert is a party animal who dislikes being alone and craves human company. The extreme introvert is a loner who prefers solitude, and is uncomfortable in many social situations. Most people are in between—about two-thirds are neither one nor the other.

You can suffer regardless of your place on the introversion-extraversion scale. And even extreme introverts need social connectedness. You could be on a solo round-the-world yacht trip with no radio, and be socially connected. This is because you'll know there are people who think of you as important in their lives, and you carry them around with you in your heart. As advance reviewer TA Sullivan stated, if I go away, I am connected to those "whose life I disrupt; who miss me on a day-to-day or week-to-week basis."

So, when your Depression tries to isolate you, resist by involving yourself with other people. Distract yourself from your woes by taking an interest in the lives of others. That's what I did as a youngster: I collected "lame ducks" who needed my help, so I could worry about them instead of myself. Fight back by doing random acts of kindness, enjoy the play of little children. If face to face contact is more than you can cope with for now, use the internet.

Here is a secret. When you avoid people, it's typically because you're scared of being judged. Actually, most others are so busy being the stars in their own inner shows that they spend little or no energy in judging you. To them, you're a walk-on extra. Instead, their attention is on assessing how others (including you) judge them.

If you go into a new situation, some people will ignore you. Ignore them. Some may react to you negatively. Their loss. But there will also be people who react with friendship and kindness. They are your future teachers and supports. Smile at them. Be open, by saying quietly, "You know, being here terrifies me. All I want to do is to run out the door, and I'm here as an act of courage." If you have picked the right person to say something like this to, the reaction will delight and uplift you.

It's far easier to move into a new group if there is a common purpose. This could be anything: church, a sport, hobby or skill, a course of study, activism to advance a cause... If you have a passion or an interest, find others who share it with you. Cooperate with them. Once there is a connection, go out of your way to be useful and of benefit to the others. Friendships will build.

The most useful group you can use is Toastmasters. On the surface, this is a group that enjoys public speaking, which I know you find scary. However, it's actually group therapy for self-confidence and inner poise. Most members start with a strong fear of speaking in public. Within a year, they do so with verve. You can also achieve this.

Meaning

Two or three times a month, I get a desperate email from a young person. Here is the best of them, with only the name changed:

> Hey, Bob, my name's Crissie, I'm 15, and I desperately need your help, although I have to admit, I feel guilty loading a stranger with my problems. I feel guilty loading them on anyone at that. Anyway, here's my problem: I have no joy for life. I don't believe in any god, I'm an atheist, and life seems totally pointless to me, and completely devoid of meaning.
>
> I'm turning 16 next week, and frankly I'm amazed I've made it thus far without jumping in front of a bus. I feel numb, and worthless, and empty. I think I'm having what people call

an existential crisis, and, now that I've reached it, it feels like the ultimate truth, that all those things I enjoyed in the past were distractions from the pointlessness and absurdity of life and existence.

I wouldn't care if I were alive or dead, and I've felt this way for well over a year. I feel like every day I'm alive is just a depressing wade through time, which doesn't exist anyway, it's just a concept, an illusion like everything else, like romance, and society, and purpose.

I want to be a psychologist when I grow up, if you manage or care to persuade me that there is something to live for, because I feel like I'm in touch with the madness. No one understands me, they can't see the bigger picture, they can't see their existence from a higher perspective, but I guess it's better that way, because then they can get lost—no, remain lost—in the oblivion, and not worry about these things and enjoy life. It's too late for me though. And I'm a mess. I'm impatient, and I can't have small talk, I can't bear to have to think about things that now seem completely irrelevant. Everything seems superficial and shallow, and I've lost trust in the world—but perhaps trust is a euphemism for naivety.

Everything seems so predictable, and stupid, and selfish and cruel, and insane. The reason I'm telling you all this is because, after what I've read on your website, I think you're the only one who could understand me, and I really hope you do. I feel so alone, and everyone is turning out to be disappointing.

so, goodbye, I hope you reply
much love, genuine love,
from me

We ended up exchanging many emails, some even years later when she was at University, studying psychology. Here is my first reply:

Dear Crissie,

What you don't realize is how intelligent you are. I suspect, just from this brief note, that you have the ability to do anything you put your mind to.

This has (rightly) led you to question all the falsehoods of society, including the hypocrisy of those who claim to worship God but do the opposite of what their religion commands.

Most people who go through an existential crisis do so in adulthood. You have reached this turning point before 16 years of age. This is an amazing achievement.

Now it's time to move forward.

By the way, I don't mind you asking me for help. I feel privileged that I get such calls of desperation several times a month, and often I am able to make life a little easier for the other person. In my everyday life, people pay me in order to deal with similar issues, but there again, my joy is in their success, not in the money I earn (although that's useful for paying the bills).

Based on the evidence you have considered so far, you have rejected religion. But that doesn't mean that life is meaningless and has no purpose.

Suppose there was no God, nothing but us, as byproducts of existence. Well then, we are still capable of creating meaning and purpose. If there is a God, and God is good, then my purpose in life is to be the best human being that faulty, limited little me can be. If there is no God, then the best thing I can do is still to be the best human being I can be.

A potato grows deep in the forest. It sets flower, but the flower bears no seed. All summer the flower is there, but no one sees it, not even a bird. Comes the autumn, and the flower dies.

It was still beautiful. It still existed, and had a right to that existence.

To be a good psychologist, it is necessary to have suffered. Otherwise, how can you have empathy for sufferers? You can do no good by being superior and pitying, only by feeling equal to your client, although farther along the path to a good life. So, look on your current stage as an apprenticeship. You're learning what it is like to feel depressed, to drift rudderless, so that later on, once you have finished your education, you can help others.

Crissie, I also reject organized religion. And I don't believe that there is a Father in the Sky, a Person who pulls the strings of earthly puppets. But I have found a great deal of evidence that there is a God, that there is purpose and meaning. God is not out there, but within your heart and mine. It is the God within you that looks at society and rejects the craziness. Since that's all you have encountered in your short life, you have rejected everything. But there is more than greed and selfishness and aggression and competition. There is also selfless giving, and hope, and beauty. Look around you. Apart from the creations of humankind, we live on a beautiful planet. And us humans have created beauty too, in visual arts, and music, and dance, and the music of words.

So, Crissie my dear, don't look for meaning and purpose out there, supplied by someone else. Do what I'm doing, and look within your heart. It is there.

For me, part of the meaning of my existence is all the kids in the world. You're all my grandchildren.

Bob

By coincidence (if there is such a thing), I got a cry for help a week later, from a British medical student. His issues were so similar that I sent the same answer to him.

My words pulled both these fine young people out of their dark hole. The student wrote:

> I never thought of it like that, that my suffering now is what can help me in future. I spent so long worrying about whether or not there will be a tomorrow or a future or is my lifespan ending. But as this has been going on for so long (about 8 months) I am now beginning to realise just how much time I have wasted in worrying; worrying that, in hindsight, has been pointless. If I had spent more time focussed and less time worrying, indeed that time could have been used so much better. So, I found it very encouraging to look at it in that way, that all this will only serve to make me a better doctor myself.

I hope my words give you some guidance, too. My final email to the medical student said, "My friend, you can pay me by passing the love on when it's your turn to be a teacher." And the same to you, if you should find solace and help in this book.

Homework

- Whatever Depression tells you, do the opposite.
- Fix up your sleeping pattern.
- Change to a good diet.
- Form the habit of regular antidepressant exercise.
- Have fun; get a good laugh.
- Regularly do things in a creative way.
- Form or strengthen social networks.

- Read *Man's Search for Meaning* by Viktor Frankl.

Remember, it's DOING that works, not reading about it. But do continue reading while working on these first-aid issues.

3 Relaxation and Meditation

As we have seen, a relaxed body and a clear, peaceful mind are necessary for good sleep. They're also excellent tools in their own right, and they feel good. They are physical pain relievers, make us cope better with the stresses of life, and are essential tools for the next step beyond merely relieving depression: they assist us to becoming better than "normal." Also, stress interferes with digestion, raises blood pressure, and shuts down the immune system. Regular relaxation and meditation are essential holidays from the craziness of "normal" living. In addition, learning to relax specific muscle groups is useful when exercising.

Muscular Relaxation

There are many methods for learning to relax your body. Most of them derive from the work of Edmund Jacobson, an early 20th century physiologist. Here is the version I have used and taught for many years. This is a two-stage process. Learning the technique takes about two weeks of daily practice. At first, a session lasts 15 to 20 minutes. Later on, you can speed up, but why hurry, since the exercises feel pleasant and do you good?

At the end of the two weeks, you'll also have created a tool for yourself that can relax your whole body with a single thought.

Learning stage

Choose your environment carefully while learning. Once you have an established skill, you can relax your body in almost any set of circumstances. But at first, make sure you'll be undisturbed, and as free from pain and discomfort (full bladder, hunger, cold, heat etc.) as possible. If you wish, you can play relaxing music to mask distracting noises.

Get comfortable. A reclining chair that supports the back of the head is good. Lying on a firm but soft surface like a carpeted floor is the best, unless you have difficulty with lying flat, or with getting up afterward. A bed tends to be too soft during this learning stage. Many people find that small cushions under the knees and head increase comfort. Your body temperature will drop during relaxation, so wear loose, warm clothes and perhaps cover up with a rug.

You'll need to memorize the order of exercises. You can record them, or have someone else read them for you the first few times.

Each exercise involves the following:

- Take a comfortably deep breath and hold it. Unless it causes pain, breathe so your abdomen rises and falls rather than only your chest.

- While holding the breath, tighten the relevant muscle group. Concentrate on what muscular tension there feels like.

- As you breathe out, say "LET GO" (or a keyword/phrase of your choice) within your mind. Relax the tension in the relevant muscle group, and concentrate on what it feels like now. Compare it to the previous feeling of having it tight.

Do each muscle group twice. If you notice tension anywhere you've already relaxed, go back and "let go" again. There are 16 groups. This means that during a session, you will relax muscles and associate this with breathing out and saying "let go" 32 or more times.

As far as possible, concentrate all your attention on the current exercise, on the sensations within this muscle group. If any thoughts or external distractions intrude, allow them, but just ignore them.

Here are the muscle groups I use, and instructions for tensing and relaxing each:

- **Left hand and lower arm:** Make a fist, like squeezing a lemon. To relax, open the hand and let everything flop. Your fingers become limp, uncooked sausages.

- **Right hand and lower arm:** same with the right hand.

- **Left upper arm:** Leave your lower arm where it is, relaxed if possible. Bulge out the muscles of your upper arm like a male model or bodybuilder (or Popeye after eating spinach). When it's relaxed, feel how heavy your lower arm becomes.

- **Right upper arm.**

- **Left lower leg:** Tighten the calf muscles by pointing your toes like a ballerina, but be careful not to get a cramp. When it's relaxed, feel how soft and warm the leg and foot have become.

- **Right lower leg.**
- **Left upper leg:** Straighten the leg, actually trying to bend the knee the wrong way, while pulling your foot back so it forms an acute angle with the leg. Feel the powerful muscles of your thigh bunch up. Relaxing will make your lower leg feel very heavy.
- **Right upper leg.**

Arms and legs are the easiest, so I use them to warm up. The face is the most complex, and therefore most difficult. It comes next.

- **Eyes, forehead and scalp** can be tensed and relaxed together, or separately. To tense the eye muscles, focus close, looking at a fly on your nose. To tense the muscles in forehead, temples and scalp, use an exaggeratedly angry frown: pulling the brows down and corrugating them. Relaxing the eye muscles involves looking at infinity: the mast of a ship on the horizon. For the other bits, imagine a wave of smoothness starting just above the eyes, and sweeping back right over the top. This exercise involves two lots of headache muscles, so it's good to practice it.

- **Cheeks and nose.** To tension, make an exaggerated "bad smell" grimace, flaring your nostrils. It looks ridiculous, but so what? Then, as you breathe out, feel your cheeks go smooth and soft. These muscles are involved in "sinus headaches."

- **Mouth region.** Press your tongue hard against the roof of the mouth. At the same time, stretch your lips into an ear-to-ear frog grin. Relaxed, the tongue is in the middle of the mouth. The lips touch, but the lower jaw hangs loose.

- **Neck.** Pull your head in like a turtle. Don't push your shoulders up, but shorten the neck. Particularly, feel the tension at the back. As you relax, your head will become heavy and floppy. Move it slightly around, then rest it against the headrest or cushion.

- **Chest.** You know how models pose for glamor photos? Put them up like that. Relaxing, feel the softness of the pectoralis muscles.

- **Abdomen**. Make it rock hard. When it smooths out, feel your insides relax, too.

- **Back**. If you are sitting, try to push the back off the chair. If lying, try to make a hole in the floor with your body. Push with all your back, from the shoulders to the hip. When you've relaxed it all, you may feel residual tension in some part, because the back is very complex, being responsible for balance. Repeat this exercise until there are no "steel cables" anywhere.

- **Buttocks and pelvic floor**. Ladies, imagine you have to pass water, and must stop mid-stream. Cut it off. Gentlemen, this doesn't work for us. Cut off the back end instead.

If any step hurts, skip it.

Having done all this, stay there a little longer. Keep breathing, nice and slow and deep. With each exhalation, think at a different part of your body, and let go of any residual tension.

This set of exercises will have significantly lowered your blood pressure, so don't stand up immediately. First, move head, arms and legs around a little.

Using the Skill

As you continue your practice, you'll find that you can relax larger and larger chunks of your body, for example both your arms together, and your entire torso. By the end of two weeks, breathing out and thinking "Let go!" will relax all your body instantly.

You now have a stress-management tool for the rest of your life. Any time you want to reduce anxiety, control anger or worry, all you need to do is to breathe deeply, and think "Let go!" as you breathe out.

At first, use it only in mild situations such as annoyance at being put on hold on the telephone. As you become more practiced, you can use the tool in more challenging situations, like waiting for a possibly painful medical procedure, or for a job interview.

The tool is useless once strong emotion grips you. You need to remember to use it at the early stages. If you try and it fails, you weaken it, but that's not a great drama: you can re-learn it in a few pleasant sessions.

Mindfulness Meditation

Mindfulness is a matter of concentration, of attending, rather than of relaxation. It has become very fashionable over the past forty years or so. It has an ancient history in eastern cultures, but is also part of the western tradition, by different names.

Dr. Ian Ellis-Jones has explained this perfectly at https://tinyurl.com/bobrich03. It means simply accepting what is, focusing on the present moment, doing any activity with full concentration on it.

> I know the thought is quite absurd,
> but it'd be fun to be a bird:
> to soar above the treetops high,
> and fly under a plain blue sky.
>
> Birds are people with little brain --
> and that's a great plus, let me explain.
> Troubles and sorrows do not last,
> but soon become the distant past.
>
> The joys of NOW fill all the world --
> it's quite clever, being a bird.
> Come to think, you don't need wings
> to get such a good view on things.

That's it. This little poem came to me in 2001, and has been my solace many a time.

Here is another analogy. Suppose an infant is using me as a receptor: this baby senses whatever perceptions, thoughts, memories, emotions, bodily sensations I have. Only, for the child, they're absolutely novel and new. So, they are novel and new for me. Each experience can have the freshness of its first instance. A smell, a memory of having met someone, the look of a tree, an old tune... all of them are fresh and novel and brilliant.

I have used mindfulness as a lifesaver with suicidal clients. My novel, *Ascending Spiral*, is a fictionalized version of my own life (except that the protagonist, Pip, made the right choices wherever I hadn't, being my role model. More of this technique later.) It starts with an actual episode with a client who wanted to die.

> "Come on, Alison," I said, "we're going for a walk." I led her outside. Speaking gently, calmly, and just loud enough to be heard over the noise of the traffic, I said, "Alison, look at the sky. See the color. Don't put a name on it, just see it. The clouds. They're just shapes."

A truck went by. "Hear that sound. It's just a sound. And now the smell. Don't judge it, don't name it, just experience it. And look at this wall, that pattern on it." We walked a few steps. "Feel the pressure of the ground on your feet. Just feel it. And how your legs work. And your breath: chest rising and falling. That tree. Look, every leaf is different."

Slowly we walked around the block. Waving blades of grass... the pressure of her T-shirt on her back... the look of a rose... the crunch of gravel under our feet... the pattern a butterfly wove in the air... I focused her on Now. This moment. This instant. This.

In ten minutes, we were back in our chairs. She could now tell me of her tragedy.

Jon Kabat-Zinn started a "Stress Reduction Clinic" at the University of Massachusetts Medical School in 1979. His approach of using mindfulness to help people to cope with severe chronic pain is now famous, applied all over the world, and supported by many scientific studies. I've used it personally, and have taught it to many clients with physical pain.

It works equally well for emotional pain, or for absolutely any problem.

OK, enough of the commercials. How do you do it?

I know of twelve mindfulness techniques. All of them work equally well, although there are different effects when used for purposes other than achieving inner peace. Here, I'll extract what's common to them.

Pick an object of focus. This could be something in your body—the breath is often used, but it could be your pulse, the pain in your back (I am serious), the touch of clothes on a part of your body, or the feelings of your muscles working as you slowly walk. It could be something external—a sound, a flickering candle, ducks floating on a lake. It can be a repeating thought, which you can say silently to yourself, or chant aloud (alone or with a group of others). It can be an abstract concept like beauty, or love, or wishing someone else to heal.

Deepak Chopra has described a more challenging version: Attend to one thing, for example the leaves of a tree swaying in a breeze. While continuing to focus on this, also attend to a second thing, like the feeling of your feet on the ground. Then add a third, and keep adding. He says some people can simultaneously attend to twenty things. I've managed eight.

However, the traditional is one focus, to the exclusion of everything else.

Keep returning. Other things are guaranteed to intrude on your attention. This is often a thought, but could be a noise, someone talking, an itch, the beating of your heart when you want to attend to the breath, whatever.

Many people think they can't meditate, because they're unable to make such distractions go away. Actually, the more you try to send them away, the worse they get. This is the joke about how to make a wart drop off: stand under the light of the full moon, and for one minute, do NOT think of the word "hippopotamus." Or here is a challenge: refuse to think of what you had for breakfast.

The secret to dealing with distractions is not the attempt to banish them, but simply allowing them to be there. So, I am sitting in my chair, focusing on the feeling of air going in and out of my nose; warm going out, relatively cool going in. A thought pops into my mind: *I mustn't forget that 10 o'clock appointment!* This thought is allowed. I thank it, and return my attention to my breath. Next, a smell intrudes on my awareness: my wife must be baking cookies. Lucky me. Lucky me for having a wife—I was very lonely as a youngster. Hey, I've wandered away from my focus. Thank you, smell, thank you, wife. Back to the breath.

So, **allow distractions, but as soon as you realize you've wandered, return to your chosen object of focus.**

Actually, it is possible to make thoughts go away, and doing that is also a wonderful form of meditation, but the essence of mindfulness, its use in overcoming problems like depression, is the attend-wander-return cycle.

That's it. That's all of it. Everything else is incidental. Your posture, how you hold your hands, the object of focus, the activity you are involved in—none of this matters. To illustrate my point, here is an essay that's one of a collection I've made available as a free book, titled *You too can live in contentment*.

Walking, boring?

A friend on a writing list is trying to reduce her weight, but complained that walking is so BORING. I was cheeky enough to respond thus:

Walking can be a form of meditation.

Look around. There is a sky above. Never is it the same. Gray, blue, the palettes of the sunrise and sunset, storms and fluffy clouds on the gentle breeze...

One of the things I like about this planet is the birds.

Wonderful little people, they go about their business in a way that I find amusing, edifying and entertaining. Watch birds, and you'll never be bored.

Plants are interesting people, too. From the tiniest mosses to the mightiest trees, all are unique individuals who deserve the focus of attention. I have saved people from suicide by asking them to study the leaves of a tree—each different, each responding to the breeze in its own way, you can even say, each with a personality of its own.

There are the human things too: buildings, garden designs, children, facial expressions each hiding or displaying a story, pathos and courage and cruelty and kindness.

And all this is only vision. Listen to the symphony of your surroundings, ranging from the rhythm of your own breath to the many sounds that surround you. Even ugly things like traffic noises can be perceived as the music of civilization.

You also have a nose, and though it's not the nose of a canine, it does well enough, and with practice will pick up a lot about your world. Some of it is poetry, some, well, modern poetry, which to my mind is on the nose, but all of it is worth focusing on.

That's the outside. Within, you can go into a restful place by noting the feel of the ground on the soles of your feet, the smooth coordination of arm and leg muscles as they stretch and contract in smooth harmony.

Walking, boring?

This is also mindfulness meditation. Jon Kabat-Zinn calls it living in the nowscape.

Guided Imagery

Another, quite different way of putting peace into your heart is by going on a little inner journey. Tell yourself a story, and live it within your imagination, as vividly as possible. Actually, this is the technique of hypnosis, so, good guided imagery is self-hypnosis. This technique takes you into a trance state, which is nothing mysterious. If you've ever felt as if no time had passed, but you've done something like reading a good book, driving from A to B, or doing the ironing, then you've been in a trance state.

Guided imagery can have up to six components, but it isn't necessary to use all six.

Relaxation

First, relax your body by any suitable method. If you've already learned my technique, just think "Let go!" as you breathe out, and feel your body go soft and quiet.

Another version, particularly useful if you're in pain or unwell, is to close your eyes, and imagine a source of Healing Light out in space. This can be almost anything: God, an angel, your long-dead, beloved grandmother, a glowing planet, or an entire galaxy. One client imagined it as the dog of her childhood, whose name had been Angel.

Invite this healing light to shine on top of your head. Feel it gently tingling its way in; relaxing, soothing.

Extend the area of healing light down so it's like a cap over forehead, ears, back of the head.

Now it's over your closed eyes, soothing, healing. Down your cheeks, over your mouth and jaw. Down to your neck, relaxing the strong muscles that carry the head.

Feel the beautiful healing light trickle into your shoulders, relaxing, soothing, smoothing, so your arms get heavy. Now into your upper arms on both sides... lower arms... all the way to your fingertips.

Next the upper body: chest, back, heart, lungs. Feel them glow.

The lower body: stomach muscles, lower back, all those wonderful organs within, glowing.

Then your buttocks... upper legs... lower legs... all the way to the tips of your toes.

Top to toe, glowing, healing, beautiful within.

Induction

This is a scene, vividly described using all the sense modalities, in which there is movement and progression. The script may invite you to walk in a valley between forested mountains, with a creek chattering on your left and grazing animals on your right, along a path to a waterfall. The path leads you actually behind the falling water, onto a stone ledge. Stone above your head, stone below your feet, stone at your back, the curtain of falling water in front. Water is the universal cleanser: it cleans away all hurt and pain. It is the universal solvent: dissolves all stress and trouble.

Or go down an elevator from the fiftieth floor, watching the numbers above the door going from 50 to 1 to 'ground.' A gentle downhill walk along a forest path is great.

People who have physical handicaps do best with a script in which they can stay still. A great one is to sit comfortably in the back of a rowboat. The person you trust most in all the world is behind you, out of sight but felt. This person is gently, slowly rowing. All your pain, suffering, worries are on the shore.

You can devise your own scripts, or check out my *Healing Scripts* CD at http://bobswriting.com/psych/heal.html

Deepening

This is simply a second, different induction script. It is a short journey of some kind, like a walk down the forest path or a descent in the elevator. It ends up in your "safe place." It isn't necessary, unless you want to go really deep.

Safe place

This is somewhere you can feel absolutely the best. It can be a real place you love, or something made up in your imagination. Typical choices are a tropical beach, a mountain top, a comfortable seat by a waterfall, looking at a flower-covered cottage, being inside your childhood bedroom. You can remember, or construct, any environment you like.

But you don't have to stick with realism. Especially if your body is not a nice place to be in because of pain, you can become someone or something else. Three of my favorites are:

- Being a trout in a rock pool, gently waving my fins so I stay motionless relative to the shore, my muscular, beautiful, shining body gently undulating, perfect for my world and my world perfect for me in the cool, crystal clear water, with the silver roof of the surface above me...

- Being an eagle. My mighty wings are spread wide, motion-less as I lazily circle in a thermal updraft, far above all the pain and worry down there on the ground. I can feel my clawed feet hidden within the feathers of my body, my spread tail steering me, the calm gaze of my powerful eyes scanning the ground far below. The wind is gently ruffling my feathers.

- Being a tree. This is similarly detailed. You can take perhaps ten minutes of creation, starting from the taproots and going up to the leaves. Once it's complete, you can instantly return to it.

One middle-aged lady liked to sit on a fluff of a cloud. A man chose to look at a poster of a waterfall in Tasmania, then step through it so he could look at the falling water, hear the roar, feel the spray on his face. You can be in a rocking chair, with a toddler you love (who is perhaps an objectionable teenager now!) quietly playing at your feet.

Tie your safe place to feelings of serenity, safety, comfort, strength, power, self-control... whatever personal qualities will help you to cope with your current situation. I always make the suggestion that you will be able to access the safe place when out of the trance, at any time, while doing any other task. This is quite possible. You can be in the middle of a painful medical procedure, having an argument with someone, being cross-examined by a hostile barrister in court, or doing a complicated job, and at the same time feel yourself in the safe place, drawing strength and peace from it.

Work

You enter trance for a reason. This could be pain control, healing some illness or injury, dealing with distressing memories, or merely stress reduction.

Return

Take time when emerging from a trance, especially a deep one. If for any reason a trance is interrupted, you can develop a headache, be disoriented, and be affected by suggestions made but not cancelled. In that case, you need to return into the trance, and come out slowly.

When using guided imagery with a person, my invariable script is to slowly count backward from 5. At each count, I draw the subject's attention to some aspect of the situation: the feel of the chair against the body, breathing, the sounds around, etc.

Homework

Over two or three weeks, establish the "Let go!" habit until it automatically relaxes your body in one breath.

Practice mindfulness meditation at least once a day. A few minutes will do at first, but gradually increase. As you improve, start doing everyday activities mindfully.

Learn to use guided imagery. Find CDs or written scripts, or make up your own. A good time for this activity is when you're settling for sleep.

The Conventional View

Human suffering has been medicalized. Depression is one of many "mental disorders" classified in the International Classification of Disorders (ICD 10) and in the Diagnostic and Statistical Manual of the American Psychiatric Association (DSM 5).

I agree with critics like Gary Greenberg, who consider the whole concept to be invented. "As the rest of medicine became oriented toward diagnosing illnesses by seeking their causes in biochemistry, in the late 19th, early 20th century, the claim to authority of any medical specialty hinged on its ability to diagnose suffering. To say 'okay, your sore throat and fever are strep throat.' But psychiatry was unable to do that and was in danger of being discredited. As early as 1886, prominent psychiatrists worried that they would be left behind, or written out of the medical kingdom." (see https://tinyurl.com/bobrich02)

Giving impressive-sounding names to aspects of human suffering is an excellent tool—for overmedicating people, as Robert Whitaker states in his 2010 book, *Anatomy of an Epidemic: Magic Bullets, Psychiatric Drugs and the rise of Mental Illness in America.*

You see, a psychiatric diagnostic category is a list of symptoms. You "have" the disorder if you experience a sufficient number of the symptoms on the list.

Here is the list for "major depressive episode:" (DSM 5)

1. Depressed mood most of the day, nearly every day, as indicated by either subjective report (e.g., feels sad, empty, hopeless) or observation made by others (e.g., appears tearful). (*Note:* In children and adolescents, can be irritable mood.)

2. Markedly diminished interest or pleasure in all, or

almost all, activities most of the day, nearly every day (as indicated by either subjective account or observation.)

3. Significant weight loss when not dieting, or weight gain (e.g., a change of more than 5% of body weight in a month), or decrease or increase in appetite nearly every day. (*Note:* In children, consider failure to make expected weight gain.)

4. Insomnia or hypersomnia nearly every day.

5. Psychomotor agitation or retardation nearly every day (observable by others, not merely subjective feelings of restlessness or being slowed down).

6. Fatigue or loss of energy nearly every day.

7. Feelings of worthlessness or excessive or inappropriate guilt (which may be delusional) nearly every day (not merely self-reproach or guilt about being sick).

8. Diminished ability to think or concentrate, or indecisiveness, nearly every day (either by subjective account or as observed by others).

9. Recurrent thoughts of death (not just fear of dying), recurrent suicidal ideation without a specific plan, or a suicide attempt or a specific plan for committing suicide.

If you and/or someone observing you report the first two, plus three others, then you qualify for the diagnosis of "major depressive episode." There are a number of provisions to exclude other diagnoses.

So, "he is depressed" is shorthand for "he is sad most of the time, can't find pleasure in anything much, probably has sleeping or eating problems of some kind, and..."

Next, we can ask, "Why does he feel sad most of the time?"

Because he is depressed, of course.

Can you see the circularity?

So, the label is not an explanation, but merely a summary description. It's like saying, "He is overweight because he weighs significantly more than he should, given his height."

A diagnostic system, putting suffering in boxes, is politically and commercially motivated science fiction. The diagnosis, "Post-Traumatic Stress Disorder" (PTSD), was invented for the very good reason of validating the suffering of Vietnam War veterans. Each revision of the classificatory systems adds new disorders, has others removed. Drug companies have been shown to campaign for new markets for their products. And so on.

Another problem is "comorbidity." A diagnostic category should be, well, a category. A great deal of evidence shows it's rare to find someone suffering from "pure" Depression. In my case, when I was young, I also qualified for a diagnosis of PTSD. About 80% of people diagnosable with major depression are also diagnosable with one or more of the "anxiety disorders."

People diagnosed with all sorts of other conditions very often also "have" depression. For example, one study published in the *Journal of Urology* in February, 2018, showed that diagnosable depression and anxiety were reduced after an operation that improved men's ability to urinate and have sex.

So, a psychiatric disorder is not a category, and doesn't actually explain anything. Otherwise it's very useful... for pharmaceutical companies.

Also, while there have been huge advances in neuroscience, no DSM category has ever been validated with any biological markers.

Sorry, I promised that I wouldn't get into academic arguments, and here I am, doing it. This, however, is an essential issue. If Depression is a disease, a malfunction of the brain, a chemical imbalance, then medicines are the only solution. This is very profitable, but leaves people either suffering the symptoms, or suffering the drugs' effects, or both. That's not to say that antidepressants don't work. They do have a role to play, but at best, they ease the symptoms while you take the drug, so you can work on your problems.

However, if Depression is not something you are, and not even something you have, but something you DO, then there is hope.

Homework

Make yourself a cup of coffee, tea, or whatever your favorite non-alcoholic drink is, and enjoy it.

Sources of Sadness

There are various reasons people may have an ongoing sad mood. More than one can operate in a given situation, but even then, it's useful to understand each.

Realistic

Our mood constantly varies. It's OK to feel sad from time to time. It can be a realistic reaction to your situation. If that's the case, give yourself permission. Change is the only constant, and this, too, shall pass.

A huge kind of realistic sadness is anticipatory grief, when people see the threats to their existence. During the second half of the 20th Century, this was fear of nuclear war. That's still there to a lesser extent, but has been surpassed by environmental despair. This is the problem I struggle with, all the time. I'll teach you my tools for coping with it in Part 5.

Grief

If you have suffered a loss of any kind, you'll be grieving. This could last five minutes for an unimportant sports defeat, or up to two years for losing someone you love. (Anything longer is likely to be because you have become "stuck in grief." Read *Seven Choices*, a wonderful book by Elizabeth Harper Neeld.)

Burnout

Beverley Potter defines burnout as "Skills and knowledge remain intact, but the will to perform, the spirit within, is gone." She also calls it "job depression," which is exactly right.

It's due to emotional overload from your obligations (whether paid work or not). Those most at risk are conscientious people whose actions and decisions impact on others: doctors, nurses, psychologists, social workers, teachers, parents, policemen, etc. People in leadership roles can also suffer burnout.

This is a reversible problem. Implementing the seven recommendations in the "First Aid" chapter, plus engaging in regular relaxation and meditation will do it.

Seasonal Affective Disorder (SAD)

SAD is a reaction to long hours of darkness and long periods of gloomy weather, which people in the cooler regions of our planet experience from late autumn to early spring. This is biological, but easy to fix. The solution is regular exposure to a suitably designed bright light. SAD UK gives recommendations here: http://www.sad.org.uk/buying-a-sad-light/

Post-Partum Depression

A majority of women experience post-baby blues while their hormones rebalance themselves after the birth of a baby. Normality returns after two to three weeks. Knowing this, you can cheerfully wait out the temporary misery.

For some reason, the low mood can persist for some women, and this can be a very serious problem. A short course of medication can help, but then use the easing of symptoms to do therapy on yourself. This is easiest with a good psychologist, but some people can do it unaided, for example by using the tools in this book.

A wise precaution is to do therapy before the birth. Think of this as an insurance policy, just in case.

Chemical Causes

Both marijuana and alcohol are central nervous depressants. They can ease social inhibitions and anxieties, so that you might enjoy yourself, but the actual effect is to lower mood.

Withdrawal from methamphetamine, and drugs like heroin and cocaine, involve terribly deep depression. This is the way these drugs induce addiction.

According to a recent examination of data regarding 26,000 people by Quato and colleagues, many prescription drugs have depression as a possible side effect. The study demonstrated that when you take several such drugs, the risk of depression increases.

Meaninglessness

This is a big one. Re-read my email exchange with "Crissie" on p. 14. Also, do yourself a favor, and read three books: *Man's search for meaning* by Viktor Frankl, which I mentioned under "First Aid," *The Rugmaker of Mazar-e-Sharif* by Najaf Mazari, and *The Power of Good People* by Para Paheer and Alison Corke.

Part 5 covers how to deport Depression from your life, and is actually a manual on how to gain meaning.

* * *

There are three other patterns of ongoing sadness. I'll use the diagnostic labels, but remember, the label is only a summary for a set of behaviors ("symptoms"), not an explanation.

Dysthymia

"Dysthymia is a continuous long-term (chronic) form of depression. You may lose interest in normal daily activities, feel hopeless, lack productivity, have low self-esteem and an overall feeling of inadequacy. These feelings last for years and may significantly interfere with your relationships, school, work and daily activities" (Mayo Clinic).

Major Depression

The difference from dysthymia is one of severity. Major depresssion is more major, believe it or not. It can go in episodes lasting weeks or months, with periods of "normality" in between, or can be ongoing. I've listed the symptoms on p. 31.

Bipolar Disorder

People suffering this pattern may go on OK for much of their life, but can crash into deep depression that can be suicidal. At other times, they experience a "high," during which their thinking speeds up, they have trouble sleeping, can't keep still, their every thought feels like the product of a genius, they are loud and sometimes aggressive. Some suffer delusions and hallucinations. They may engage in irrational acts like splurging all their money, or unwise sexual adventures.

However, many people with bipolar use the manic episodes for achieving great things. There is a long list of high achievers in all fields whose success is thanks to their bipolar. Lin Edwards has described this at https://tinyurl.com/bobrich04

Unlike other patterns of sadness, bipolar has considerable genetic involvement. This is NOT a doom, but a tendency. I'll discuss causation in the next chapter.

Typically, a perfectly OK person experiences some traumatic event, which triggers a manic episode. After this, the bipolar pattern keeps going.

For example, Gabriel met a girl while he was a tourist in Britain, and they married. He returned home to rent a house and get everything ready—then she sent a letter saying she wasn't following. He got drunk, and woke in jail with no memory for the night before. He spent time for having assaulted police (broke one policeman's jaw), and from the time of that letter, had the bipolar pattern.

Medication helps with bipolar. Suitable drugs even out the mood fluctuations. However, they all have nasty side effects, so it's best to use them as little as possible, and to engage in psychotherapy.

I have a long-term friend who now controls his bipolar almost entirely using the tools I will describe later. He rarely needs to take medication, but will do so if he finds himself in difficulties.

On my website, you can read a letter from a young woman who was unable to take the medicines, and has developed a completely psychological way of coping, and more than coping but thriving: http://bobswriting.com/psych/bipolar-nodrugs.html

Her method will work for anyone willing to put in the effort, with bipolar, or with other psychological problems.

Homework

Think about each of the patterns I've described, and consider whether it applies to you. Use the internet to read up on any that do.

The Causes of Human Suffering

Heredity and environment

People are complex beasties. Behavior, including thoughts and emotions, is the result of a very complex network of causes. It's not a question of heredity vs. environment, but, for any particular event or tendency, the intricate interaction of many hereditary and environmental influences.

No investigator has found a gene, or collection of minor genes, for any "mental disorder," including depression. All the same, each of us has a pattern of genetic strengths and weaknesses. My genetic profile makes me safe from delusions and hallucinations, and I don't easily get anxious. Put enough pressure on me, however, and I become sad, withdraw from human contact, feel hopeless and apathetic.

There is an interaction between genetic weaknesses and how we respond to pressure. To understand this, look at something simpler like alcoholism. Some rare people can get drunk every day for years, until their liver and brain are destroyed, but if they can't grab a drink, they don't suffer withdrawal symptoms. There is no chemical addiction. At the other extreme are people who are hooked after getting drunk once. Most of us are in between. This is the genetic component. The environmental part is of course whether you indulge, how badly, and how often. Even the most susceptible person will avoid alcoholism by staying sober.

Similarly, some people will simply never get depressed. When they suffer losses, they experience grief, which is a normal reaction. When they see someone else in a terrible situation, they may show empathy by feeling sad for that person. However, regardless of the pressure life puts on them, they never react with ongoing low mood, withdrawal, apathy, loss of energy, etc. They break in another direction, such as explosive violence, or addictive behavior, or ongoing, gut-wrenching anxiety, or hallucinations and delusions, or of course a mixture of several of these.

Others are so susceptible to experiencing the depressive symptoms that they fall into the pit at very little provocation. They are rare;

again, most of us are between the two extremes.

Depression runs in families, but this isn't evidence for heredity-only. As little children, we model on the important people in our lives: parents, siblings, teachers, other kids. That's why "Do as I say, not as I do" doesn't work. My grandfather's reaction to being sent to the Ghetto was an attempt to kill himself (which in retrospect may have been wisdom). As a toddler, I absorbed the emotional atmosphere, even if I didn't have much understanding of words yet.

Here is an interesting fact: when people adopt a baby, they somehow choose one who will grow to resemble them even in physical characteristics. But then, haven't you occasionally seen the same with pets?

If your potential weakness is to become depressed and you have a child, natural or adopted, chances are that child will grow into an adult with the same vulnerability.

Homework

You can't do anything about a genetic tendency to react to overwhelming pressure with depression, but you can simply accept this pattern. It's no worse than the others.

Examine your family history. Identify the people whose depressive reactions you learned to model on, the particular memories of events that taught you that this is the way to react to pressure. Then find other role models, and self-consciously, deliberately copy them. This can be an ongoing project for years.

Childhood Trauma

A huge body of evidence links adult "mental disorders" to verifiable abuse and/or neglect in childhood. For example, John Read and his colleagues reviewed a large number of studies in 2005. This paper has become famous for demonstrating that schizophrenia has a causal relationship to childhood abuse, and the more severe the abuse, the worse the condition in adulthood. "Patients subjected to child sexual abuse or child physical abuse have earlier first admissions, longer and more frequent hospitalizations, spend longer in seclusion, receive more medication, are more likely to self-mutilate and to try to kill themselves, and have higher global symptom severity."

In one study, suicidality was better predicted by childhood abuse than by a current diagnosis of depression.

The same is true for other diagnoses.

As if that wasn't bad enough, this kind of evidence only examines what a child protection agency would consider abuse/neglect. In fact, what matters is the child's subjective view of the situation, which results in belief systems that poison the rest of that person's life. Such a belief system, positive or negative, is what Aaron Beck called a "schema" and a "core belief." His cognitive therapy is very powerful, because it works on changing negative schemas.

The problem with abuse is not the events that happen, but their effects on the child. In 1991, Lenore Terr defined childhood trauma as "the mental result of one sudden, external blow or a series of blows, rendering the young person temporarily helpless, and breaking past ordinary coping and defensive operations." Let me emphasize, the trauma is the mental result, not the event.

Here are three examples of such "blows" from among my clients.

Giles came for help because of a relationship breakdown. He was 52. Six months before, Shirley separated from her abusive husband. As always when encountering people in trouble, Giles did everything possible to help her. After a strenuous session of furniture-moving, she put her arms around him and gave him a thank-you kiss.

"That's my first kiss, ever," he told her.

So, she took him to her bed, and into her heart, and into her life.

Giles knew from the first moment that it couldn't last. He cherished and served Shirley with every thought and action, but continuously grieved in advance for when she'd tell him to go.

After six months, Shirley said, "Giles, I'll love you till the end of my life, but I just can't live with the gloom anymore." She ordered him to get therapy for his depression. If he could fix it, she'd gladly have him back.

In the first session, he calmly told me, "It's hopeless. I knew it couldn't last. My mother is 83. I need to stay alive for her, but when she dies, I'll kill myself."

I used a standard "cognitive-behavioral" technique to gently lead him to where the hopelessness came from. He reported a memory of when he was eight years old. He came home from school, to see a moving company truck in front of the house. Dad said, "Get in the car. We're moving."

He'd been happy at school, with lots of friends. He never met those friends again. He was happy in this neighborhood. The thought occurred to him, *They didn't bother to tell me in advance, because I don't matter.*

This idea then permanently changed his reality. When something bad happened in his life, it proved that he didn't matter. When something good happened, he reacted in one or more of these ways:

- Didn't even notice
- Explained it away as luck, or someone else's kindness
- Knew in advance that it couldn't last.

He spent all of his life in service to others. They mattered; he himself didn't.

Did uncovering this belief cure him? Of course not. Understanding in the head never does. But it was a first step.

Cyril's trauma occurred when he was five. His father took him horse riding for the first time. There, he overheard one bigger boy saying to another, "That little kid Cyril is not much good."

Being only five, with no previous riding experience, of course he was no good at horse riding. He, however, took it in another way, as an overall description of what he was, rather than referring to a particular skill.

He grew into an attractive, tall, muscular young man with a very impressive list of academic, sports and work achievements. Whatever he did, he did better than anyone else. He never let any young woman emotionally close, because he knew they couldn't continue to like him once they discovered the "real Cyril," the one who was not much good. Every day, he obsessively disproved the belief, and every day, he needed to do so again.

Because this was not a rational belief, no amount of arguing with him would have shifted it. Helping him needed an entirely different set of tools.

When **Raelene** was seven years old, her family moved to a new place that didn't allow dogs. Her parents found a home for their dog with relatives, and Raelene often spent weekends with the cousins, and her dog. All the same, deep within, she KNEW: you're guaranteed to lose anyone you love. As a teenager and young woman, she was often approached by decent, attractive young men, but she pushed them away. Caring for someone was too dangerous.

You will also enjoy a short story at my blog: "Defeating the Blood-Red Dragon" https://tinyurl.com/bobrich05

Can you see the pattern? THIS is where depression comes from.

Homework

Later, I'll show you how to identify negative "core beliefs" that poison your life. However, it's more powerful if you manage it yourself without instruction or help. Can you find the thoughts that come to you whenever the sun goes out in your world? What are they, and where do they come from?

Now you're an adult, can you smilingly let go of these irrational beliefs you acquired as a child?

Society

Population Pressure

As I said at the start, depression is a rapidly increasing epidemic. Understanding the reasons will allow you the choice of refusing to buy into the craziness, and I hope, turn you into a campaigner for a sane culture.

The first thing is to learn about the work of John B. Calhoun. He spent a lifetime studying the effects of population pressure on rodents. His early work was to construct naturalistic rat or mouse colonies, supply them with unlimited food and water, and watch them breed so their habitat became increasingly crowded. The colonies died out, although always supplied with plenty of food. There was a sequence of symptoms.

First came increases in what we consider stress-related diseases: cancer, asthma, eczema, digestive ulcers, high blood pressure with its complications of stroke and heart attacks. Not every rat suffered, but many did, their numbers rising with population pressure.

The next development was that some females were neglectful in raising their young. Rat behavior is largely learned, and many in the next generation didn't know how to be normal rats. This is like "personality disorders" in humans.

Finally came two patterns: aggression and apathy. Some rats became very territorial. Both females and males killed babies. Some males attacked anyone entering their space, even their mates. Armies of males fought wars to the death. This got so bad in some colonies that infant mortality became 96%.

A great many rats, particularly males, reacted by withdrawal. They sank into what in humans could only be described as major depression.

However, there is encouraging information here as well. At each level, there were unaffected rats, who reacted in normal, rational ways to their circumstances.

Later in his life, Calhoun worked on looking for solutions to dealing with population pressure. This was less successful.

Calhoun became a social activist, and his research was taken up by people who wanted to change society. The academic response was to dismiss his work. Writers like Ramsden and Adams approved of his scientific research, but almost ridiculed its extension to implications for humans. But... look around our world. You'll find an epidemic of stress-related physical disorders, including cancers. There is a more serious, unacknowledged problem with so-called personality disorders: culture is disintegrating. But most important, there are two frightening trends exactly predicted by Calhoun's work:

1. Insane violence. Endless wars, genocide, the nuclear posturings of Trump, Putin and Kim, terrorism, police shootings, domestic violence, school massacres, many people fantasizing about killing strangers for no reason (and a few actually doing it), on and on... My novel *Hit and Run* is the story of the redemption of such a person http://bobswriting.com/hitandrun.html

You'd be surprised at how many teenagers of both sexes I've helped out of urges to kill. The idea revolts them, but won't leave them alone. I have posted a page at my website with links to twenty such questions-and-answers: http://bobswriting.com/psych/murderurges.html

2. Giving up. Depression is increasing globally, and is likely to overtake other sources of disability in a few years. Addictions of many kinds are also a way of giving up, as are head-in-the sand denial, and retail therapy. These are also growing epidemics.

For rats, crowding is the other rats they smell, see and hear. For humans, it's other people who have negative impacts on us. When a car worker in Detroit or a call center person in New York becomes unemployed because of outsourcing, then the millions in Asia provide crowd pressure. When a Californian knows that terrible droughts and wildfires are nature's response to increasing greenhouse gases in the atmosphere, that's crowding. When we hate and fear people a little different from us, wars and terrorism and cruelty are crowding.

Some rats weren't affected, until the very last. Some humans also choose to stay rational, compassionate, and decent. As I'll show you, deliberately making the choice of treating all other humans as our brothers and sisters is one of the major defenses against depression.

It is interesting that warfare as we know it started when humans formed concentrated groups. Hunter-gatherers necessarily live in small groups that meet from time to time. When animals were domesticated, a nomadic lifestyle meant that a large area was used by a group that could be much more numerous. They needed to be aggressive in order to defend their territory for the use of their animals. This is crowding, despite the apparently open spaces. Agriculture produced much more food, leading to villages, towns, cities—and organized warfare.

The difference is clear when you compare hostilities among traditional people in the New Guinea highlands with Australian Aborigines. The Papuans in New Guinea live in villages, and, according to Tim Flannery, have possibly been farming for longer than anywhere else in the world. Ongoing "payback" is an inherent part of the culture. People from one village raid the neighboring one, killing someone as vengeance for a past act of aggression. Then, the victim village hits back, on and on. I suppose this can be considered as a population control mechanism, but not one I approve of.

In contrast, Australian Aborigines were hunter-gatherers until very recent times. Each nation were carers for, and inherent parts of, a particular area of land, which even today they think of as their mother and their being. Others could only enter their land with their permission. Conflicts did occur. For example, one Queensland nation had the custom of raiding neighbors. But "warfare" consisted of the two groups shouting insults at each other, then a few spears were thrown. Typically, someone was speared in a leg, and that was the end of it.

We can't return to a hunter-gatherer lifestyle, but we can learn from the attitudes that went with it.

Our society induces aggression, discrimination, genocide on the one hand, and depression, retail therapy, anxiety, gambling, and substance abuse on the other, because we are experiencing the Calhoun effect. I think John B. Calhoun should get a posthumous Nobel Prize.

The Damaging Myths of Global Culture

Here is a magic wand for you, loaded with one wish. What will it be?

OK. Whatever it is, why did you wish for that?

Most people's answer is some version of "It'd make me happy."

Why do you want something to make you happy?

Isn't that a stupid question? Isn't that what we all want?

The *happiness myth* is highly damaging, and a major cause of unhappiness.

There are many instances illustrating that the meaning of life can be a variety of other values:

- **Serving God.** Mother Teresa spent her life in serving the poor of Calcutta. The martyrs willingly fed the lions in the circus of Rome. Terrifyingly, people willingly use themselves as human bombs, today.

- **Serving Country.** People volunteer for likely death or injury, undergo extreme hardship, when their country is in a war they believe to be just.

- **Advancing an Ideal.** Think of Gandhi, Martin Luther King, Mandela and their sufferings. Malala Yousafzai was shot in the head because she wouldn't stop campaigning for girls' right to an education. There are journalists, and political opponents of dictatorships, in prison right now. Environmental protectors have been assassinated.

Imagine this. Someone you love (child, parent, partner, pet) is in a burning house. I'll grant your every wish for a year if you refuse to save this person. What will you do? I don't know anyone who'd make the selfish choice.

Why does striving for happiness cause unhappiness? Because happiness is not a state that can be maintained. People don't "live happily ever after." When things are better than usual, you feel happy; when worse, unhappy. Change is the only constant, so happiness and unhappiness also change. This is the experimentally well-supported concept of "hedonic adaptation."

First, let's define adaptation. It's when something initially attracts your attention, but soon fades from consciousness. You walk into a room, and note its smell. Very soon, that awareness is gone. My daughter once lived in a house near a railway line. While visiting her, I recoiled when the house started shaking, and a loud noise drowned out every other sound. "Oh, that's terrible," I said when it passed.

"What?" she asked. She hadn't even noticed the train thundering past.

I am sure that now you can think of many instances of adaptation from your own life.

"Hedonic" means having to do with pleasure. So, "hedonic adaptation" means getting used to a particular level of positive or negative set of circumstances. Because of hedonic adaptation, the benefit of anything positive or negative quickly wears off, returning you to your long-term set point of perceived wellbeing. Win millions of dollars in a lottery, and you'll be on top of the clouds—for a while. Soon, though, the new normal will be just normal, and your habitual mood returns to what it was before. Or, say you suffer an accident resulting in physical handicaps, pain, perhaps disfigurement. You'll find that after a while, although the situation is permanent, your long-term mood will be much the same as previously. If you've always been a cheerful, positive person, you'll cope with new your situation in a cheerful, positive way. As I write, I have a dear friend who is gradually dying from motor neuron disease, losing various bodily functions all too rapidly. She is an inspiration to everyone who knows her, because she is determined to get the best out of however few days are left to her.

Imagine a man whose habitual, long term mood is sadness. He wants to be happy, so buys a car. This works, but the happiness won't last. The new toy will soon be merely part of the background, and no longer give him a jolt of pleasure. Remembering that buying the car had made him happy, he may now trade it in for an even better one. That works... for a while. In 1971, Brickman and Campbell described this as "a futile and desperate hedonic treadmill."

Seeking happiness is an addiction. You do something that lifts your mood, but once the effect wears off, you need to repeat the action, exactly like, say, a cocaine addict.

This leads us to the *consumer myth*: that happiness can be bought. I guess it's always been around, but it is now the major device for running the economy. Buy our gizmo! How can you be happy unless you enjoy our holiday! You MUST keep up with the latest fashion! You're ugly unless you wear our makeup!

If buying were to permanently make us happy, we would buy once, then stop. Therefore, CONSUMER SOCIETY IS BASED ON NECESSARY, REPEATING AND ONGOING DISSATISFACTION.

So, people spend money, often money they don't have. Therefore, they need to earn money, which is fine if they enjoy their job, but wage slavery otherwise.

From the start of the Industrial Revolution, we've had a growing system of consumption. Everything is focused on making the money go around.

In the same way as individuals can become addicted to whatever gives them temporary happiness, we have an entire global economy addicted to growth.

Suppose that a great many people buy the absolute minimum they can. Instead of meeting their needs by buying products and services, as far as possible they grow their own food, build their own house, make their own clothes and furniture, and so on. They cooperate with others, supporting each other, and they barter skills and time. They generate their own entertainment, and do their best to surround themselves with beauty. Rather than aiming to possess as much stuff as possible, they aim for a complex, varied life with people they care for.

They'd be sabotaging the economy. Their lifestyle would destroy jobs, make goods and services more expensive for everyone else, and worst of all, fail to pass wealth to the 1%.

Therefore, it's necessary to convince everyone that this is a bad idea, that they need to buy goods and services. There are many tools for this. Planned obsolescence ensures that new, better models make your current possession seem useless in comparison. Gizmos need to fail sooner than rather than later, and it's best if they are not repairable. Of course, the advertising industry is a very successful means of brainwashing people to keep buying. Even entertainment pushes the hidden message that you must be dissatisfied with what you have, so you will keep the wheels of industry turning.

Consumer society is built on dissatisfaction. Contented, happy people buy less, so everything needs to make people discontented.

However, there is worse than the consumer myth. The *romantic myth* extends it into the realm of personal relationships. People dream of the happiness they'll gain when they meet their soulmate. Seeking the perfect partner is a selfish wish: "I want someone to make me happy."

Love that lasts a long time, and is likely to make you feel contented, is different. In contrast to such taking love, it is giving love: "I want someone to love." If two people have this attitude to each other, and both are in the relationship in order to make the other happy, then you have something wonderful.

The problem with the romantic myth is that it seeks the perfect love. When problems arise, as they always do, people realize that, no, this relationship isn't perfect after all. If the consumer myth has been generalized to people, then the obvious reaction is to trade in on a new model. This is a major reason for the high divorce rate. Nearly half of all marriages end in divorce, and subsequent marriages are more likely to fail. That's not even counting couples who live together without officially marrying.

There is hope. You needn't buy into the myth. Go to http://anxietyanddepression-help.com and look for "How to have a good relationship." There, I summarize a great deal of information that'll help you to live contentedly with the one partner, although not "happily ever after."

The final myth is that *more is better, without limit.* It is not only responsible for depression, but also for the destruction of the entire life support system of our planet.

Research shows the opposite. Having less than you need in your circumstances is hardship, but too much also gets in the way of a good life. The perfect amount is as with food. A healthy eating pattern is when you're well nourished, but eat less than you could hold. Similarly, the right amount of wealth is when you avoid hardship, but need to struggle and strive to meet some of your wants. Then achieving your goals results in pleasure instead of being a "so what" blip.

The problem is not wealth as such, but considering it central to your existence. In my novel, *Guardian Angel*, Gerald, a minister of religion, explains it like this:

> "When Jesus said it's difficult for a rich man to enter heaven, he actually didn't mean the wealth, but the attitude it engenders. Wealth is an obstacle because it becomes an addiction. The more you have, the more you want. You manage to have an acre of land? You want ten. If you have ten, you think you need a hundred. You can only satisfy this desire by competing against other people. Even if you're invariably honest, your gain is someone else's loss, exploitation and often even suffering. So, you cannot serve this master and also give the love of your heart to all who live, and to their Master. However, if you have wealth but refuse to be addicted to it, God will welcome you in heaven."
>
> "I've never heard it explained like this before." The captain looked thoughtful. "That saying about the eye of the needle has always sounded like something thrown out to keep poor people in their place and not covet wealth."
>
> "Yes, that's how the princes of the church use it, and priests follow. But Jesus befriended rich people and poor, regardless, so he couldn't have intended that. He was, as I said, against greed, not against happening to be rich. Joseph of Arimathea was a rich man, and yet he has been venerated all through the ages."

Wanting more wealth than you need can affect you in several other ways:

- Focus on wealth isolates people, same as any obsession. If you want to be with cheerful, helpful, cooperative people, you'll find them among those who can meet their needs, but have no excess possessions to worry about. Tourists to poor countries are often amazed at the friendliness, love of fun, and welcoming cooperation they find there, compared to the mutual mistrust and aggressiveness so often found in (over)-developed countries.

- For many people, level of income, amount of stuff, is a competitive issue. There is always someone worse off to treat with contempt or condescension, and someone better off to envy. You can never find contentment if life is a race without end.

- When you focus on possessions, there is no such thing as "enough."

- Often, high income has a cost. Virginia was the Principal of an exclusive K-12 girls' school. All the Best People sent their daughters there. Her students included those with brilliant results in academics, and in every other field. She had a high income, and a high standing in the community.

She made an appointment, and told me she couldn't stand it anymore. She loved teaching; contact with students, but rarely saw them. It was all administration, bureaucracy, politicking, fundraising, conflict resolution, buttering up wealthy parents and alumni.

I told her about burnout, but she answered, "It's more than that. Eight years ago when I started, it was a challenge and a joy, but I simply don't want to spend the rest of my working time doing this."

I asked her to brainstorm about what else she might do that would maintain what she valued about her job, and removed the objectionable parts.

She canceled the second appointment, and I thought I'd failed her.

Six months later, she sent me a lovely email:

Dear Bob,

I cannot thank you enough for what you did for me. I've resigned, and trained up my replacement. Got a job as an English, Geography and History teacher in a State high school, at a quarter of my previous salary, and it's like coming alive again. I inspire my students (well, most of them), have the joy of organizing the annual school play, and have the time for fun in my life again.

Bless you!

Virginia.

* * *

What I've explained concerns the individual, but a second problem with too much wealth is where it comes from, and what damage you do in acquiring it.

A major reason for dread, despair and unhappiness for many people is that they accurately see disaster looming. For an even larger number, this knowledge is there, but suppressed, denied, unacknowledged. That denial takes tremendous effort, which makes people tired, reduces their motivation ("There is no point to anything. Why bother?"), leads them to turn to activities like gambling, addictions, expensive holidays—anything to focus on other than the danger. Such people either ignore the facts, or are missionary in their spirit of denial. Those facts cannot be true; are due to a conspiracy, or based on false science, or whatever. It goes something like this, not in thought-out words, but underneath consciousness: "If that were true, I'd have to make complete changes in how I live. If that were true, my loved ones would be in terrible danger. So, of course it cannot be true."

As I said, the global economy is healthy when people are chronically dissatisfied with their lives, so they'll buy, buy, buy. But also, it can only stay healthy if it keeps growing. How well the economy is growing is assessed by looking at growth in the Gross Domestic Product (GDP).

I learn a lot from fictional characters I've invented, who then take on a life of their own. One said, "If I were an evil genius and wanted to design a system to cause maximum misery while destroying life on Earth, I'd construct the GDP as the measure, and economic mechanisms that collapse unless GDP keeps growing."

Earth is a limited system. The only thing that grows without limits in a limited system is cancer. The global economy is a cancer that is well on the way to killing its host.

This book is not the place to go into the details, but if you visit my blog, Bobbing Around, at https://bobrich18.wordpress.com, you'll see the evidence. Read the essay "How to change the world." The facts are also readily available in many other places.

I am not only talking about climate change here. We are also officially in the sixth great extinction event of this planet, with species dying out, on latest evidence, 1000 times the expected rate; and global economic collapse is looming, and only staved off with smoke and mirrors tricks.

I know this. (Or, OK, if you disagree, I fully and honestly believe my doomsday delusions.) All the same, I manage to live a contented life. If I can, you can.

Homework

Examine to what extent, if at all, these societal pressures have affected you in the past. Take your time—weeks of thought, journaling and investigation are OK.

Are some of your negative actions due to population pressure in the sense I've described?

Have you bought into any of the myths of society? Have they harmed you?

Can you choose to react differently?

The Development of Resilience

Resilience is the ability to bounce back. Some people are fragile. When they crack under pressure, it takes a great deal for them to recover, if they ever do. Others are able to recover very quickly. As with other psychological characteristics, part of it is no doubt genetics, but, again, modeling is hugely important.

Prosilience: Building your resilience for a turbulent world by Linda Hoopes is a handbook on how to make yourself more resilient.

Also, improving your resilience is part of what I'll teach you later.

Enclose a newly planted tree seedling in windproof surroundings for a couple of years. When you remove the protection, the first breeze will snap off branches, and a wind that'd make other young trees sway will shatter this one. This is because when a tree stem or branch is still young and flexible, its movements in the wind cause little fractures that heal, producing scar tissue that makes the tree strong. So, overprotecting the baby tree stops it from being resilient later.

I remember reading about a famous dog experiment when I was a student. Only, that was in the early 1960s, and for the life of me, I can't find the reference.

Like-sex litter mates were assigned to experimental or control groups. Controls were given to families as normal pets.

The experimental dogs were raised in doggy heaven: every wish granted, protected from all illness, all frustration, all pain.

After two years, the experimental dogs were given to families matched on a number of factors to their litter mate's.

All the experimental animals died within six months. Some died from infections because they didn't have antibodies, but most from depression. When a meal is delayed, your dog may complain, but will get over it: eat the deferred treat, then get on with life. For these cosseted animals, it was a major tragedy that took them days to get over. A normal dog will shrug off minor injuries. The experimental dogs found the slightest pain intolerable.

So, they couldn't cope with real life. Sadly, it killed them.

Children should be raised like the control pups: treated with kind but firm discipline, and allowed to experience the rough and tumble of normal puppy life.

So, here, as with wealth, we have an example of the Buddhist concept of the golden middle. Childhood abuse leads to adult suffering. Overprotection leads to vulnerability. Perfect parenting is the golden middle: rules imposed with firm but loving discipline. It's unconditional love and acceptance, while allowing the child to learn from mistakes.

It is clear rules, firmly enforced, with unconditional love, and the complete absence of physical and mental abuse. But you don't have to be perfect. Parents are allowed to be human.

You may enjoy reading my little essay on cat love and dog love: https://tinyurl.com/bobrich06. Then there is a short story: *Armour-coating our kids* https://tinyurl.com/bobrich07

Homework

Now or later, you may want to read *Prosilience: Building your resilience for a turbulent world* by Linda Hoopes.

Again, I am setting a task I will give guidance on later in the book. It'll be more powerful if you can invent it for yourself.

Do you have thin skin, what my wife describes as long toes (easy to step on)? Does the slightest bad luck drag you down? Do you find it difficult to overcome even minor adversity?

What can you do to toughen up? Devise a method for becoming more resilient, and try it out. Major habit change takes about three weeks of conscientious practice. Give it a good go, and see if it improves your life. If it's not as good as you've hoped, tweak it and try again.

This is what I did for myself when I was a terribly depressed young fellow. It worked for me.

In the meantime, read on: next we explore techniques for controlling depression.

5 | Controlling Depression

Nothing works for everyone, but something works for everyone.

That's to say, even the most effective, most powerful techniques fail for some people, but everyone can find something helpful. Only one thing makes you helpless: the belief that nothing can help. Belief is immensely powerful, so get your mind around this:

THERE ARE THINGS THAT WORK FOR YOU.

In this Part, I describe several techniques and approaches. Research shows each to work for many people. Some have a success rate approaching 90%. When you give one of them an honest go, it will probably be helpful. Even if it isn't, don't toss it in the trash. All things are change—it may well work for you the next time. Research also supports this.

Also, you'll notice that they overlap. That's OK, and it makes learning them easier.

You may well feel tempted to skip ahead to the next Part, where I describe how to get rid of the depressive habit set altogether, but resist the temptation. Those activities are based on these control techniques, and progress is cumulative. The tools I teach you here are essential. Learn them and apply them.

I won't give a complete catalogue of therapeutic approaches, because the ones below are more than enough. Some, like Emotion-Focused Therapy, are excellent, with good research support, but difficult if not impossible to do as self-therapy. You can read an excellent description of emotion-focused therapy here: https://tinyurl.com/bobrich08

Others have considerable overlap with the ones I have included.

Fixing the thinking

Emotions, thoughts, actions, bodily sensations form a plate of spaghetti. They're all tangled together. There are forms of therapy that address each of these.

However, thoughts are more accessible for most people, and easier to modify, than other aspects of experience. And habits of thought and action are easier to change than habits of emotion. This is the basis of cognitive-behavioral therapy (CBT).

Identifying Damaging Beliefs

The Downward Arrow Technique

Raelene (p. 40) came to me because, at 25 years of age, she'd never had a steady boyfriend, far less a partner, and she'd finally given in to her mother's nagging to do something about it. She was a remarkably beautiful young woman. One look, and I was sure the problem wasn't lack of applicants. She was also doing postdoctoral research, competed in athletics, and had a wide group of both male and female friends.

First, I asked her if she had any objection to a romantic bond with someone. (Some people do.) She liked the idea and missed it, but said with a laugh, "I've tried dozens of times, but it never lasts." She'd tried a lesbian relationship, but it ended within weeks, just like the ones with males.

I had her fill out the Beck Depression Inventory, because I didn't have a clue why she was in this situation. Her score indicated moderate to severe depression. Like I'd been earlier in my life, she was a high-performing person carrying the dreadful load of persistent sadness.

We needed to find the automatic belief(s) that dragged her down. I had to start somewhere, so asked, "Please tell me about the last time you went on a date."

"Oh, Paul? He is one of my training buddies, a champion hurdler. He's been coaching me on technique ever since I came to this university." (Naturally, I won't tell you which one).

"How long have you known him?"

"About six months. And before you ask, he's been making signals at me all that time."

"And?"

"And I put him off. You know, settling into a new place, new job, new research project, no time for such nonsense."

"But at last you went out with him?"

"My mother came for a visit, and happened to meet him." She

laughed. "If she was thirty years younger, I reckon she'd have jumped at him. Told me not to be stupid, and give him a go. So, I did."

"Did you enjoy yourself?"

"No, or I wouldn't be here. I kept thinking, this will spoil a good friendship."

"What does it say about your long-term thinking to have the thought that a date with Paul will spoil a good friendship?"

"Let me think... He has many good qualities, and there is the risk that I may fall in love with him."

"Suppose you fall in love with him. Why is that a risk?"

"Because such things never last. When we break up, it'll always be between us."

"What does it say about your long-term thinking to have the thought that such things never last?"

"Hmm. That I expect a relationship to always break down."

"What does it say about you that you expect a relationship always to break down?"

She looked ready to cry. "It's terrifying. I'd rather stay safe. You always lose whoever you love."

This is the downward arrow technique, repeatedly but gently probing deeper through asking essentially the same question. It led us to a highly damaging core belief we could now work on.

You can use it on yourself. Suppose you consider enrolling in a course of study, but think, *Why risk failing? It's safer not to.* OK, ask yourself what's so bad about risking failure. Whatever your answer, keep probing downward, until you get at a basic, self-sabotaging belief you can put into words, perhaps for the first time. Now you are ready for self-therapy.

Or an acquaintance may have walked past you like you weren't there, and you found yourself furious. This is an opportunity to unearth a damaging core belief. Sit down somewhere quiet and ask, "I got angry that Carol ignored me. What does that say about me?" Repeat this a few times, and you could find something like, "I must have everybody's approval all the time. It's terrible if I don't."

Homework

Look up "downward arrow technique" on a search engine, and watch a couple of the several video examples that'll come up on the first page.

The ABC diary

Attention is a searchlight. Whatever it shines on stands out, while everything else recedes into background. Attention is also a fertilizer. Whatever you apply it to grows, while everything you withdraw it from withers away.

The "ABC diary" is the most frequently used tool in CBT. The letters stand for "Antecedent" (what went before), "Behavior," and "Consequence" (what happened because of the behavior). It's an exploratory device like the downward arrow, but is also a powerful changing tool in its own right, because it forces attention on what you want to achieve.

My second client as a beginning therapist was a lady with a food obsession. Whatever she was doing, she vividly imagined eating ten chocolate bars in a row, or spooning down a whole container of ice cream, or a jar of honey. This happened about five times a day. She had an iron will, so didn't actually indulge, but the obsessive thoughts gave her a lot of distress. I told her we needed to track down where these imaginings came from, so set her up with an ABC diary:

Date and time	Circum-stances	A (activity)	B (food thought)	C (emotional reaction)

At the next session, she reported that the food thoughts had reduced a great deal. She'd only spotted three in a week! Since she had obsessive tendencies, I was certain this was an honest count. Later, she went through the Christmas period of traditional gluttony without being tempted to overindulge, for the first time in many years.

This is how an ABC diary works. If you monitor something unwanted, it reduces. If you monitor something you want more of, it increases. Magic.

I've used versions of it for all sorts of behaviors. Mario was scared of failing, because he "mooned off" during study. I got him to note the time he started studying, and the times when he noticed that he was thinking about something else. His study time increased, distracted time practically disappeared.

It's almost a bonus that this kind of record also acts as a detective tool. For example, over a week's tracking of when her mood plummeted, Claire noticed that this was whenever she saw someone else being happy. The typical thought was some version of "Not fair, why not me?" As we discussed this, she had a vivid recall of her mother screaming at her, "You're such a miserable little bitch! Why can't you be happy for a change?"

Bingo. I gently asked her, "How long will you put up with your mother's abuse?"

This had never occurred to her before. "OK, what should I do?"

"Brainstorm. Design a thought you'll deliberately think when seeing someone happy, and say it to yourself in such situations."

She eventually came up with "Bless you for being happy."

This was highly successful, after a couple of weeks of invariable practice. It illustrates one of the findings I'll explore in Part 5, that the more you give, the more you get.

Homework

Pick a habit you find distressing, and set up an ABC diary for it. Record instances for a couple of weeks, then study your diary for patterns. Note any changes in its frequency.

Look for recurring patterns that make sense of the habit.

Clarifying Questions

This is one of Aaron Beck's best inventions. He devised it to deal with the MAJOR source of conflict between people, what he calls "mind reading," but I have personally applied it when the problem was between me and myself. I've taught it to countless clients.

Mind reading happens because we don't perceive facts, but our interpretation of them. Here is a short story I wrote about it, based on an actual client couple:

Coffee storm

Retirement has its routines.

Every day after lunch, Celia consumed the next of an endless succession of romances. John snoozed away while supposedly playing online scrabble. Then, at four o'clock, Celia made them a cup of coffee each.

Today, John woke with a start and looked at the clock: nearly 4:30. Wanting to do something nice, he asked, "Would you like me to make the coffee?"

"Wait a minute." Celia sounded annoyed. She stayed silent for awhile, then snapped, "I'll do it, but CAN'T YOU WAIT TILL I FINISH MY CHAPTER?"

Feeling both puzzled and hurt, John shouted back, "DON'T BOTHER!" He stormed off to the kitchen, and made one cup of coffee, for himself.

That evening, Celia set the table for one, and had a poached egg on toast, with nothing for John.

He'd never hit her, or any other woman, but sure felt like it now. To control himself, he stormed out, bought a hamburger, then visited their daughter, Mandy, crying on her shoulder about this incomprehensible reaction to an attempt at kindness.

"Sit down, Father," Mandy commanded, and pecked on her phone. She put it on speaker.

"I knew that passive-aggressive wannabe manipulator would run straight to her favorite daughter," Celia's voice came.

John opened his mouth in outrage, but Mandy waved him to silence. "Mother, can you explain what you mean by that?"

"OK, so I was caught up in a great book and was a few minutes late with the coffee, but couldn't he just have said so?"

"Father, what did you say?"

"I saw she was enjoying her book, and offered to make us the cup. And she bloody bit me in the bum!"

"Liar! You mocked me!"

John spoke loudly, to ensure Celia heard him: "Mandy, you've got an opportunity for a live-in babysitter and domestic worker. You know I'm a good cook when I put my mind to it. May I move into your spare room?"

"Jee, what a child! So you're going to divorce me because your coffee was a half-hour late!"

Mandy eventually convinced them to see me for couple therapy. What was going on here?

John made a genuine offer, but what Celia heard was a passive aggressive hint, "Hey, you're late with your job. I expect to be served on time." *How arrogant!* she thought—and reacted.

In session, I said, "Celia, your interpretation was perfectly possible, but was in fact incorrect. John honestly offered to take over the coffee-making. He was offering an act of friendship, and got attacked for it. How else could you have handled the situation?"

She looked angrily at me, and seemed ready to walk out. "So, it's all my fault?"

Oops. I'd put my foot in it. (Therapists aren't perfect, either.) I realized that mind reading was probably a well-entrenched negative habit of hers. "Not at all," I answered. I am not looking at assigning fault, but at helping the two of you to design a new way of enjoying each other's company. But OK, John, you go first. When Celia snapped at you, you reacted with anger and outrage, and retaliated. Can you think of something you could have said that'd have saved the situation?"

"Uh... no."

"You were really and genuinely offering to make the coffee. How could you get her to realize that?"

"By telling her."

"And?"

He grinned. "And bloody making two cups."

Got him. Now I returned to Celia. "OK. When John offered to make the coffee, you saw him as being manipulative rather than actually meaning it. Is there anything you could have said to test this theory of yours?" (This is "reframing:" I was gently leading her from certain belief to considering her interpretation as a theory. I often reframe my own internal statements.)

She shrunk in on herself for a moment, then looked me in the eyes. "Yes please, love."

Both of them came up with perfect reactions that would have eliminated the issue, but I wanted them to learn a more general tool, so switched into teacher mode, explaining about clarifying questions. Celia could have demanded, "Are you really offering, or is this a way to manipulate me to be on time with my servant's job?" John's answer should have been, "I don't look on you as a servant, and REALLY offered to make the coffee."

Similarly, if Celia had exploded, he could have used the clarifying question: "Celia, what makes you think I wasn't really offering to make the coffee? Stay there, I'll do it straight away."

I've gone into such length because you can do this with yourself.

Anne and I are in the middle of organizing a business transaction. I couldn't get through to her on the phone, and she didn't answer my emails. "She's lost interest," I thought, dejected.

She phoned today, full of enthusiasm, and explained that her phone ran out of credit, and since she is moving house, she simply didn't have the opportunity to recharge it, and her computer is still packed away...

My interpretation was wrong. I could have saved myself all that angst.

Suppose that when I had the thought that she'd lost interest, I'd questioned it. "Could there be any other explanation for her silence?"

I'm sure you can come up with several possibilities, phone malfunction being a likely one. Just for fun, see if you can generate five.

When the negative emotion is in response to someone else's behavior, a good habit is to ask the clarifying question from that person. But asking yourself is equally powerful. For example, suppose you're assembling flat-pack furniture, and find a nut missing. You get angry at shoddy packaging, and are about to phone the retailer to tell them off. It's a VERY good idea to search a little more, remembering that dropped objects can go a long way. You'll probably find it several feet away, like in a dark spot under a couch.

Remember, your reaction is to a **theory** you've formed in response to the current situation.

Homework

Next time you are angry at someone, or your mood crashes because of some happening, ask yourself, "What is my interpretation of this situation? It may be true, but what other possible interpretations can I think of? Is there any way of testing which is true?"

From Feeling to Thinking

Only, that's hard to do, isn't it? When things go wrong, we all experience emotion: become angry or anxious. That means that we react exactly as if we were facing a physical danger, and switch to "flight or fight" mode. (Actually, this is flight, fight or freeze mode. If the threat is overwhelming, we cannot act at all.) This is so well known that people talk about feeling adrenaline in the blood, which is nonsense: you don't feel adrenaline. You feel elevated heart rate, rapid, shallow upper-lung breathing, muscular tension such as hands forming fists or the jaw clenching, much quicker reaction times, enhanced vision and hearing, and very rapid, concrete thinking. All of these are admirably suited for instant physical action—and entirely unsuited to dealing with a conversation, or reading a disappointing letter, or "knowing" that you'll fail that exam tomorrow. Such situations need rational, considered thought, which is impossible in emergency mode.

Of course, by now you have a first-aid tool: take a deep breath, and as you release it, think "Let go." Only that's unlikely to work if you're already in the grip of strong emotion. So, here is a toolkit: activities that turn emotion down, and reasoning up.

How to fight a problem

1. If something works, do more of it. If it doesn't work, do something else.

2. Everything occurs in a context:

- **Where** is the problem most likely to occur?
- **When?** (time of day, day of the week, an occasion such as an anniversary)
- **Who** else is there?
- **What** are you doing at the time?
- Are certain **thoughts** or **feelings** associated with the occurrence of the problem?
- Is it **preventing** you from doing something you're **relieved** not to have to do?
- What are the **benefits** of **suffering** the problem? (e.g., do you get more attention, can put off a difficult decision, or what?)
- Is the occurrence of the problem **predictable**? Can you tell when (under what circumstances) it will strike (or get worse), when it will leave you alone (ease off)?
- Is it **controllable**? What can you do to influence it?

3. Problems feel "universal," as if they were "always there." Find exceptions: they are the clue to ways of fighting back.

4. Scaling questions

1 (low)   10 (high)

- What is the worst possible outcome of the current situation? On a scale of 1 to 10, how likely is that to happen?
- What is the best possible outcome? Rate it too.
- What is the most likely outcome? Rate it.
- How controllable is it? (1: random and unpredictable. 10: under your control).

5. Imagine you're **advising someone else**—cousin, neighbor, colleague—who has this problem. What will you suggest?

6. Keep an **ABC diary** (see p. 55). You may be tracking an action (yelling at my kids), a thought (I hate being a loser), an emotion (fear, worry, depression). All of these are "behaviors," even the ones other people can't see. The behavior may be something specific, or one of a class of things, e.g., any thought that makes you crash back into grieving.

Set down:

- when, where, with whom you were
- what happened immediately before the target behavior occurred (the trigger)
- unless you are tracking one specific behavior instead a type of behavior, write down what the behavior was (e.g., the specific thought)
- what was the consequence of the behavior (e.g., how did you feel after, what effects you had on other people).

As I said, an ABC diary is in itself a behavior change agent. Sometimes, it is the only action necessary to eliminate a bad habit. It is a source of information allowing you to plan an attack on the distressing problem. And it makes you into an observer, so that you can distance yourself from unwanted emotions.

In fact, all these techniques make the problem less pressing and immediate. Once you have engaged in one or more of these activities, you will be able to think (relatively) calmly and rationally. Then, you can ask your clarifying questions, or whatever you judge to be constructive.

Homework

Memorize this toolkit, and apply it whenever the opportunity arises. This is not as overwhelming as it may seem. Note that the list is on p. 60, so you can easily return to it. Also, you can go to http://anxietyanddepression-help.com and find it as "How to fight a problem" in the navigation bar on the left of the page. Get one of the tools clear in your mind, practice it until you're competent with it, then progress. There is no hurry, and you can read on meanwhile.

Find the trauma

Remember, on p. 38 I explained where depression comes from: it is a child's negative, self-bashing interpretation of a "blow" or series of "blows." Often, the relevant episode is easily accessible to the sufferer, and examining it through the lens of mature hindsight is very helpful. My first task with Giles, (p. 39), who was too miserable for Shirley to tolerate, was to lead him to remember the start of his lifelong troubles.

"So, let me understand this, Giles. When your mother dies, you intend to kill yourself. When was the first time you decided to do this?"

"When she had a mini-stroke, I can't remember what the doctor called it."

"A TIA?"

"That's it. I realized, she is getting old, and won't need me forever. This was before I met Shirley, and... before I lost her like I knew I would." He looked ready to cry, but put on a calm face. "No one else cares the slightest whether I live or die, so, why not?"

"Are you certain? Surely you have friends?"

"Nah. Not a one."

"If I did a survey of all the people who know you, what would they say?"

Shrug. "They don't know the real me. Yes, I'm of service whenever I can, because they matter."

"THEY matter? You don't?"

Another shrug, and a nod.

This was obviously a core belief. We were getting somewhere. "When was the first time you felt as if you didn't matter?" (This is reframing a belief taken to be true into an "as if.")

"I've known it all my life."

"Right. You crawled out of the womb believing you didn't matter?" (Again, I reframed "knowing" into "believing.")

He laughed with me. "Of course not. Wait a mo. When I was eight, one day I came home from school, and a moving company truck was standing in front of the house..."

After this, we had something to work on.

You can do this for yourself. I did. As a youngster, my self-description was, "If there is a wrong way of doing it, or even if there isn't, I'll do it that way first."

At this time, I still hated my stepfather, and often had flashbacks to his abuse. One day, I was driving along, following directions to visiting a nice family who had invited me for dinner, when, as usual, I got lost. *Oh, hell,* I thought, *if there is a wrong way of doing it, or even if there isn't, I'll do it that way first.* I pulled over to check the street directory. (For people who now follow directions on their phone, that was a book of maps you had to wade through to find your route.) "Where did that thought come from?" I asked myself.

I was transported back to an earlier time. I felt being in a kid body, kneeling on the carpet. Spread out in front of me was my brand new Meccano set, a birthday present from my grandmother. As I was puzzling over what had to go where, the door opened, and HE stood there. HE said, "Save us from the idiots of the world! If there is a wrong way of doing it, or even if there isn't, he'll do it that way first."

That flashback was a big part of the start of my healing.

So, find the thought that pulls you down the most, and identify the exact episode when it intruded into your life, then question it with adult eyes.

Who knows why Giles's parents didn't tell him of the impending relocation? It was negligent, but probably they were under multiple pressures, and just assumed he knew. I am certain it wasn't because they thought he didn't matter. That was a little boy's inaccurate interpretation.

Why did I buy into my stepfather's abusive assessment of me? Because I was a nine-year old child, and he was a powerful adult. I rejected everything about him at the time, but he colored my world anyway. That's how abuse works.

To the present day, it's actually true that I get things wrong the first couple of times I try something. Nevertheless, when I was 21, I noticed another fact about myself: "If someone else can do it, I can learn it." I can. After a few repetitions of the new activity, I understand it so well that I can teach it to others.

There was no basis of fact to Giles's damaging core belief, unlike in my case. Both of us, though, used other facts to fight the poisonous belief. During therapy, he eventually generated the thought, "I've been helping everyone all my life to prove that I matter. So, this belief turned me into a good guy people like."

Homework

Look out for your self-abusing inner clichés. If you can, track one back to an episode like Giles and I did, imagine yourself back there, and examine that young person's plight with tolerant adult love and sympathy.

Getting in its way

My sister-in-law told me she is annoyed at a habit of hers: she counts everything. Her solution: as soon as she notices, she rapidly repeats the last number in her mind, while continuing the activity. This of course means that she loses count. Then she triumphantly laughs at herself.

She doesn't know she reinvented a CBT tool. You can do this with any habit, for example occurrences of the thought, "Oh, I hate myself!" Construct a competing thought. Remember, my riposte to "If there is a wrong way of doing it, or even if there isn't, I'll do it that way first" is always, "If someone else can do it, I can learn it." Depending on your history, culture and beliefs, you might choose something like "Jesus loves me anyway," "I forgive other people, so I can forgive myself," or "Bullshit, that's only an inside noise unless I believe it."

The requirements are: you need to honestly believe the new statement, even if the old, harmful one is true (like mine); you should find it easy to remember; and apply it every time the harmful thought is triggered. If you forget, then OK, no harm done. Do better next time.

You will speed up the process, again, through keeping records. If like most people, you're welded to a cell phone, open a little file in there, and keep count of how many times each day you succeeded in using the new habit to shout over the old one, and how many times you've caught yourself slipping back. Remember, attention is magic.

Later, I'll introduce another way of dealing with self-damaging thoughts and memories, but developing an interfering habit is very useful, all the same.

Homework

Just do it.

Dealing with Secondary Gains

Every problem has some benefits. Depression is no exception. This is not to say a sufferer deliberately pretends, or makes matters worse. All the same, there are payoffs.

This is best illustrated with physical pain.

Fiona was a 43-year-old mother of two. She had suffered migraines for decades. As part of a complex attack on the problem, she analyzed her family's reaction to her suffering. She found that when she had one of her headaches, the children didn't squabble. Usually they did. Husband and kids took over almost all the household tasks. At other times, she needed to argue and cajole to get them to do their fair share, even though Fiona had a full-time job.

She didn't develop a headache in order to gain considerate, caring attention from her family. Nevertheless, it was a fact that this was what she always got when a migraine struck her, and never when she felt well.

Part of her cure was to reengineer family dynamics. All four members of the family signed a contract, involving the fair distribution of household tasks. Husband and kids agreed to "reward mom for NOT having a migraine" instead of rewarding her for having one.

Fiona also learned how to identify the triggers for her headaches: to spot early warning signs. She then took analgesics before the pain struck, and used relaxation techniques to short-circuit the mechanism of a migraine. But removing the secondary gains was a big part of her success.

OK, can you think of possible payoffs for acting depressed? A payoff is the reward that might come your way, e.g., getting out of something you'd rather not do, receiving sympathy, or being able to withdraw from a situation. Once you have gathered enough information, you can then get rewards for defeating the problem rather than rewards for suffering it.

After I wrote this section, I posted it on my blog, with a request to my friends to suggest rewards for acting depressed from their own lives, or those of others. This was very educational for me. I only received one explicit suggestion. Margaret Goodman wrote, "Some people... can be rude and cruel, then claim that the depression made them do it."

Instead, there were several strongly felt descriptions of depression from the inside. Jean, a friend and colleague I deeply respect, put the problem with my request the most clearly:

> Problem is, depression constricts your thinking. It is almost impossible to see outside the box of despair. If the depression were mild, or intermittent, it would be possible. But a full-fledged clinical depression, no. It would take a compassionate, tactful, and patient outsider to point out the benefits. Hopefully you, in your book, will be that person to many others. The only benefit I experienced from years of unremitting depression was validation that there was truly something wrong with me.

Her blog is at http://ra-info.org/

I have banished my depression decades ago. Now that I look back, I can see the secondary gains it used to get me. But I have to agree with Jean. If someone had asked me to spot them back then, I probably wouldn't have managed it. Nevertheless, getting out of that box, and seeing my behavior from the outside, would have been a great liberation.

So, let's use one of the tools of the problem-solving kit on p. 60. Do you know anyone else who is struggling with depression? Suppose that person came to you, asking for advice on spotting secondary gains.

Here is a small selection of the kinds of things you'd look for in helping your friend:

- "Oh, I can't do it" means the person can get out of trying.
- Self-harming and suicide attempts attract notice, when nothing else has.
- "I've slept in again. Oh well, no point going to school this late."
- "I just couldn't get to sleep last night, then I kept waking up. Sorry, I can't concentrate."
- Wearing his sad, hopeless face usually induces Mary to do kind things for him.
- Acting grumpy gets others to tiptoe around him, which gives him a sense of power.
- When she locks herself into her room, she usually gets out of her household tasks.
- Saying "Oh, I am so tired!" often results in Jim doing most of her share.
- Those wretched girls don't bully her when she spends lunchtime sitting in a quiet corner somewhere, doing nothing.
- People leave him alone when he strides up and down just to get rid of energy. (This is "psychomotor agitation" in the list on p. 31.)
- "A sure way to get reassurance is to cry and say it's all my fault."
- When she fails at something, she gets confirmation that she was right: she truly is hopeless and useless.
- He doesn't have to put up with all that empty chatter and socializing when he chooses to isolate himself.

If you can spot patterns like this in someone else's life, you may spot some in your own.

This then gives you enormous power: the ability to see yourself from the outside at least to some extent, and for a time. Each occasion you manage it, you grow.

The next step is, there are probably people in your life who know you well: those you live with, or used to live with, those you spend many hours with at work, and so on. Some of them are people you can trust to be kind. Ask them to help in the way I've described for your analysis of someone else's patterns.

Your helper might spot that she tends to be kind to you when you can't eat much dinner. Be thankful for that, but also, the two of you can use this new insight to ensure the kindness will not be tied to lack of appetite in the future.

And the logical follow-up is, "What else may I be doing to fish for kindness?"

You have climbed out of being a helpless prisoner in the box, and are now an active agent in reengineering your life.

Homework

Observe other people you know or suspect are depressed, and look for secondary gains they receive for specific behaviors like those I've described. There is absolutely no need to tell the other person about this, unless asked.

Pluck up your courage, and ask people in your life to help you to find rewards for the various symptoms of depression.

Once either of these activities have helped you to identify a secondary gain, set up an ABC diary to track it. For example, you might notice that "Whenever Tim has his room tidy, Mom expects him to help with the housework. When his room is a mess and he sits around with a hangdog face, she tidies it for him and lets him get away with not helping. OK, does this apply to me?" So, you'd have the ABC diary for when Mom eases off on you about helping with chores. What behaviors of yours is this associated with?

Rewriting your story

Ricky was one of those children you're glad lives in someone else's family. At school, he often bullied smaller kids, "just having fun" without any empathy, any understanding that the victim didn't enjoy the activity. He saw every word as an insult, and when he could get away with it, he retaliated with violence. His older sister often wore bruises in response to comments or actions other people would never have found offensive.

His mother dragged him into my office (almost literally). He sat in his chair, glowering at the floor while she described life with Ricky, and her and her husband's worry that he was a criminal in the making. As she said that, the expression on his face reminded me of the cliché, "If looks could kill."

"Hey, Ricky," I said, "I bet you a dollar I know what you're thinking."

"Bull... Bulldust. Yeah? You're on."

"It's not fair. She is always picking on me."

He did look at me, surprised. "Yeah. She is."

I laughed, reminding myself that even he deserved love. "Keep your dollar all the same, or use it to buy your sister something nice. Does everyone pick on you?"

No answer, but his body was a coiled spring, waiting for the punchline he could interpret as an insult.

"I have magical abilities, and can tell you why that is."

Was that a smile on his face?

"You've got a habit of sending out dark energy. Without realizing it, you've been sending out dark energy, and people respond to that. You can change that to silver energy, and people will also respond to that."

"You're making fun of me." The truculent expression was back.

I laughed again. "That was an example. You just blasted a big beam of dark energy at me. I expected it, or I'd have reacted with anger."

"Dunno what you mean."

"Let's do an experiment. Just imagine, you're walking down the street, and four teenage hoodlums jump out of a doorway. They're about to bash you up when a police car comes around the corner. The hoods run away. A policeman and policewoman get out of the car. Do you feel like thanking them?"

"Yeah, I guess I would."

"OK, pretend your mom is the policewoman. Look her in the eyes, give her your best smile, and thank her."

As he did, he looked like a nice kid. "Right, Ricky, store away what that feels like. That's sending silver energy. When you do that, people will like you, and go out of their way to do nice things for you. When you send dark energy, you'll find that everybody is your enemy."

That was only the start. The next step was to convert the family from conflict to cooperation: "Mrs. Smith, your family needs to be Ricky's support group. Changing longstanding habits is difficult. When he remembers to send silver energy, please all notice, and reward him with a smile, an appreciative word, some privileges, whatever. When he slips back, as he will because we all do, simply say some version of "You're not doing this anymore," or "That was a bit dark," or some other gentle reminder. It's important not to respond to dark energy with aggression, criticism, rejection or fear, but only with the reminder, so Ricky will remember to trick people into liking him by sending silver energy."

This is one of thousands of ways you can apply the principles of

Narrative Therapy, which was developed by Michael White and David Epston. Its central idea is:

The person never IS the problem. The person HAS a problem.

A problem is something you have, not something you are. You don't need to change your nature. You need to fight the influence of the problem on your life.

All of us must select from the huge amount of information the world throws at us all the time. We need to organize what we see, hear, feel and remember into a meaningful "story" or "picture." This always introduces biases: we notice and remember things we find interesting, important, and in line with our beliefs, expectations and prejudices. We ignore, forget or play down things that are contrary to the way we see the world. So, things we notice and remember tend to confirm and strengthen our story about ourselves and our world.

This is fine for most people, because they're OK within their story. Problems arise if you're in a story that makes you or others unhappy. Examples are stories involving beliefs like:

- "I am a violent person, have a short fuse (and can't help it)."

- "I am no good, useless, have no worth, nobody could possibly love me."

- "The world is a terribly dangerous place and I am helpless in the face of its threats."

They all involve the belief that "there is something wrong with me."

Narrative Therapy is a search for events that disprove these beliefs. There are ALWAYS exceptions: events that occurred but didn't fit the story, so were ignored, played down or forgotten. They can be used to "write a new story," one that separates the problem from the way you see yourself. Once the problem is found and named, it can be fought. In the process, you don't need to change. You discover a past, an identity, that was always there, but hidden by the biases of the previous story. The new story liberates you from the shackles of the problem.

With Ricky, I invented a reason for his perception that everyone was always insulting him, getting at him, putting him down. Instead of a need to defend himself and counterattack, I gave him a tool for making people react positively to him. This interrupted the endless cycle of his story, and allowed him to experience the joys of pleasant social interactions.

I did this for myself, and you can copy me. My problem was

depression rather than aggressiveness, but the principles are the same.

As a kid and teenager, the reality I created for myself was that I was stupid, ugly, a stuffup who couldn't do anything right, and of course no one could ever love me. Everything I did was a futile attempt to disprove this story, but I needed to disprove it every day, even every hour. Logic, reason had no effect.

Then I learned about Narrative Therapy, and decided that those terrible thoughts about myself were not MY thoughts at all. When I was a little boy, a monster moved into my brain. He was very, very good at imitating the voice of my own thoughts. It was a Misery Monster: it fed on sadness. When it managed to get me sad, it feasted and grew strong, so its aim was to gobble me up, imposing as much misery as possible.

For a while, I kept a written record. When I had the chance, I wrote my thoughts down, and examined them. Some were clearly Bob thoughts, others equally clearly monster thoughts.

If you go back to the start of the First Aid chapter, you'll see that I use the language of Narrative Therapy there (Michael White called this "externalizing language," because it makes the thought external to the person). "Whatever depression tells you, do the opposite" identifies Depression as the source that alien inner voice, not a part of you but a malicious invader.

Also, isn't this like the ABC diary? It causes change through the focusing of attention, and it uncovers negative thoughts. In fact, I call Narrative Therapy "CBT in a clown suit." It is very much more fun, and can be applied to all of the cognitive-behavioral tools I've described. While I am not setting this as formal homework, you may enjoy rereading the previous chapter, and translating each of the tools into externalizing language. For example, devising a new habit to conflict with the old one becomes "shouting over the monster."

Narrative Therapy is not a set of techniques, but a way of thinking. Although much of the scholarly writing on it is very difficult, in practice it's easy. So, I don't feel I need to say any more here. You can use any techniques, including the ones from CBT, and things you invent for yourself, from a Narrative Therapy perspective. You'll find this very powerful, and who'd believe that therapy can be fun?

In Part 5, I'll return to how I'd used Narrative Therapy for healing myself, by changing my new story in one little additional way...

Homework

From now on, think about yourself, and everyone else, in

externalizing language. That is, when someone does something you find hurtful, separate the person from the act. And isn't this the Lesson of all the great religions?

Identify your inner monster, and learn to distinguish that invader's thoughts from your own. A formal or informal ABC diary is very helpful for this.

Act The Way You Want To Be

As I said, thinking, action, emotions and bodily sensations are all part of the one thing. CBT and Narrative Therapy focus on thoughts. Acceptance and Commitment Therapy is all about doing. The acronym ACT should be said as the word "act."

This is a mindfulness-based therapy, so by now you should be well prepared for it, because you regularly enjoy mindfulness meditation, right? Mindfulness comes in because, instead of avoiding unpleasant thoughts, emotions or sensations, we accept them and observe them without judgment. It is allowing your inner experience to be as it happens to be, without an attempt at control or struggle.

Years ago, I learned about ACT through a course run by Russ Harris. Here is his definition: "Imagine a therapy that makes no attempt to reduce symptoms, but gets symptom reduction as a byproduct. A therapy firmly based in the tradition of empirical science, yet has a major emphasis on values, forgiveness, acceptance, compassion, living in the present moment, and accessing a transcendent sense of self. A therapy so hard to classify that it has been described as an 'existential humanistic cognitive behavioural therapy'."

If you like the little I say here, you must read his book, *The Happiness Trap*, which is a complete self-help guide to ACT.

The acceptance part of the name is there because our normal reaction to having a problem is to struggle with it, to try to make it go away. Problem solving is a process of identifying a problem, and finding a way of getting rid of it. This works so well in practical matters that we automatically apply it for thoughts and emotions we identify as problems, but there, the effect is the opposite. With psychological issues, the more we try, the worse the situation gets, and this is all tied up with thoughts. So, unlike cognitive therapy, the aim of which is to change the thoughts, ACT simply accepts them.

By trying to get rid of "symptoms," we worsen our situation. Worrying about being anxious is anxiety-provoking, resenting depression is depressing, and so on. ACT starts with the paradoxical viewpoint of simply accepting what is, and that makes half the problem immediately go away. I may be sad, but no longer depressed about being sad.

A typical start to therapy is to look at your past attempts to solve the problem (e.g., of ongoing sadness), and seeing that none of them have worked. They will all have something in common: a struggle to get rid of it. When you turn off the "struggle switch," the original problem may still be there, but you'll feel liberated, having shed a huge load. Remember, "If something works, do more of it. If it doesn't work, do something else."

You Are Not What You Think, But What You Do

The second part, commitment, is commitment to a certain kind of action. This then sneaks up on you, and becomes your new "second nature."

When a famous philanthropist died, he was lauded for his many acts of charity and compassion. He was so involved in his charitable activities that, for decades, he'd passed control of his business to his sons.

How did this start? According to his authorized biography, as a young man he was ruthless in his business dealings, and in his treatment of his workers. Profit was all. This affected his reputation, to the point that he was losing business. He engaged what we'd now call a PR consultant, who advised him to make highly visible charitable bequests, support foundations for good causes, etc. He started all this good work for entirely selfish reasons: to appear to be a good guy. But the result was—he BECAME a good guy. His actions came first. The motives followed.

Socrates said, "Seem the man you wish to be." That's it.

The next technique is explained through one of Russ Harris's metaphors. You're steering a boat way out at sea, and want to approach the shore. However, every time you steer shoreward, a bunch of frightening monsters swarm out from below decks, surround you, shout at you and threaten you. As soon as you change direction, they go away.

As long as you're scared of them, and give in, and avoid steering toward the shore, you feel safe—and stay all at sea.

Suppose that when they started to carry on, you continued steering for shore regardless. You'd find that they cannot stop you, and have no power to do any harm. All they can do is to threaten. They are actually cardboard cutout monsters! And if you continued ignoring them, time and again, after awhile they'd give up.

How does this work in practice?

Agnes suffered from severe Obsessive-Compulsive Disorder (OCD). She HAD TO wash her hands exactly 17 times after doing anything she considered dirty, such as grasping a door handle in a public place. She felt forced to internally recite certain words in given situations. There were a whole lot of other must-do things, but this'll do as a sample.

She knew that terrible anxiety would strike if she defied her compulsions in the slightest.

She was referred to me soon after I did my ACT course with Russ Harris, so decided to test it with her.

I asked her to make a list of all the things she'd attempted until then to free herself from this prison of compulsions. She compiled one, of fifteen different tries. We examined them. I said, "Seems to me, what's common to them is that every one of these therapies and drugs and whatnot was intended to get rid of your compulsions. They haven't worked, so we need to give something entirely different a go."

"Like what?"

"What has been the cost of all this work to avoid the anxiety?"

"I don't have a life. Might as well be dead than live like this!"

"OK, Agnes, let's do an experiment." I waved toward the handbasin, which had elbow-activated taps, since I was renting a room in a medical center. "Wipe your palms on the floor, then immediately do whatever you need to in order to stay hygienic and safe."

As soon as she finished washing her hands the first time, I said, "Can you please come back to your chair instead of more handwashings?"

"I CAN'T DO THAT!"

"When you have that thought, 'I can't do that,' is it in words you can read in your mind, or sounds, or what?"

"Uh, it's like I said them to myself inside."

"Right. Sing them. Do you know the old Beatles song, *You can't do tha-a-a-t*?"

Despite her obvious anxiety, she laughed at me. "A singer you're not."

"No. I can't hold a tune if my life depends on it. What about you?"

She sang it fine. "My mother is a Beatles fan, and I know all their songs."

"OK, within your mind, sing the song in your mother's voice."

When she nodded, I got her to do it in the Beatles' voices, from a deep baritone, and a squeaky cartoon character's.

I looked at the clock. "Hey, Agnes, it's been eight minutes since your first handwash, and guess what, you're still alive."

Her signs of anxiety had disappeared, but now her hands started shaking, sweat appeared on her forehead, her posture became stiff. She turned toward the handbasin.

"Wait." I then told her about Russ Harris's monsters on the boat. "I distracted you, so you weren't listening to the cardboard cutout monsters. As a result, you were fine, until you paid attention to them again."

This was the start of her healing.

Values

I particularly like Acceptance and Commitment Therapy because it's values-based. Two little tricks are the "funeral oration" and the "film script."

Funeral oration

In 2011, I addressed a bunch of psychologists in my role as chair of the "Public Interest" committee of the Australian Psychological Society. I decided to do my best to inspire them:

> A report from me has been circulated to all of you. I assume you can read, so I see no point in repeating content.
>
> Instead, I want to tell you why I am passionate about working for the public interest.
>
> A standard technique in Acceptance and Commitment Therapy is to tell the client: "You've just died, at 93 years of age. One of your grandchildren is to deliver your funeral oration. Write this person's speech: what you hope will be said about YOU."
>
> What works for clients works for us. OK, let me sketch out two versions of MY funeral oration:

> > Thank heavens the old bastard's gone at last. Look out you lot, I already have a good lawyer, and my share of his millions is MINE.
> >
> > When I was young, I called him Gramp to his face, but Grump behind his back. He never had time for us, it was always screwing the most out of the next business deal.

> Or the alternative:

> > Please forgive me, I can hardly speak for crying.

Grandfather is gone in physical presence, but he'll live on in my heart until I die.

Whenever I was in trouble of any kind, a quick phone call to the old boy, a few minutes of his quiet voice, and I knew again that I could cope. Let me share with you now a few of my fun times with him, and a few of the funny times...

Which one is better?

Can you see how powerful this is? Suffering is a matter of attention. By switching attention to living a life of benefit to others, our own problems recede.

Recently, I was promoting one of my novels on a Facebook group. My task was to entertain my audience through interactive exercises. One of the questions I posed was: "I am sending you all a magic wand, loaded with one wish, and that wish cannot be selfish. Well, what will be different in the world after you've waved your wand around?"

I got an incredible response. Hundreds of people posted their wishes, some even days later. A few were silly or trivial, but almost all were in tune with my philosophy, showing that basic human nature is good.

Film script

Go into a travel agent office, and say, "I want a plane out of this town."

"Certainly. Where would you like to go?"

"Uh... I don't know."

That's not a good recipe for a trip, is it?

One way of creating a destination for your life is the film script. Design the leading character of a movie that's about your life. This person has your physical appearance and life history, but thinks and acts in the way you would like to, if only you could. You don't need a storyline for what happens from this point forward, but merely design the character. Take weeks, or even months, over writing out this person's way of handling all the problems that caused you grief, in sufficient detail so that a Hollywood star could step into the role.

Then of course, be that actor. Insofar as you can, act as if you were this fictional you.

Note what's in a movie: only things you can see and hear. Thoughts, emotions, motives are as irrelevant as they were to that philanthropist who'd died a genuinely good man.

I write novels, not movies, so that's what I did. My novel,

Ascending Spiral, is my life story, but the hero, Pip, handles events the way I wish I had, and so provides me with a role model.

As I said, I don't need to give you more detailed guides on ACT, because Russ Harris has done so in *The Happiness Trap*.

Homework

Write a funeral oration you want one of your grandchildren to deliver when you've died at 93.

Taking a lot longer, write a film script with no plot for the future, but a hero who shares your appearance, circumstances and history, and who ACTs in a way you wish you could. Do it in sufficient detail that a Hollywood star could step into the role—then be the actor yourself.

If you find ACT to your liking, read *The Happiness Trap* by Russ Harris.

6 | The Cure for Depression

The Destination

In 2009, "Tom," a suicidally depressed 16-year-old, wrote me a long and pain-filled email. He felt he had no friends, no future, no chance of ever finding love. He wasn't bullied, since he had a brown belt in Karate, but was always the last to be picked for a team, always on the outer. He believed no one liked him, and more, that no one could like him. Here is my answer:

> Dear Tom,
>
> When I was your age, I was where you are now. I had no friends. I had no family even, because I lived in a migrant hostel and my family were on the other side of earth. I was good at fighting (did judo and boxing), so physically I was OK, but I felt terribly isolated. I dreamed about having a girlfriend, but believed it would never happen, no matter how long I lived. After all, what girl would possibly love me?
>
> Now, I have a wide range of friends, people who speak highly of me. When I meet people, they always react to me with liking. Even if I walk down the street, strangers smile at me. I've been married (to the same person) for 42.5 years, have three terrific children, and grandchildren. I have a wonderful career that gives me a lot of satisfaction, and in which I am of benefit to other people. If I could do it, so can you.
>
> I was isolated and picked on until I was in my early 20s. Then it stopped. I have worked out the reason: until then I thought like a victim, and was treated like a victim. After that, I accepted and respected myself, so the energy I sent out induced others to respect me.
>
> My depression came from an abusive stepfather. I met him

again when I was 21. To my surprise, I liked the old bastard. I pitied him, so could no longer hate him. Although I didn't realize it at the time, looking back I see that this was the start of my healing.

Tom, depression is an inner monster that moves in when you're a little child. It whispers lies to you, and is very good at making you believe that these lies are your own thoughts. To be subject to depression, you need to have distorted inner beliefs in three families, and I can see that you have all three. These are:

1. "I am faulty." In my case, I just knew I was stupid, and ugly, and could never do anything right, and anybody who knew me could not possibly love me.

2. "The world is a bad place." You have this one ++.

3. "There is no hope, nothing can ever help."

These beliefs are self-damaging, and false. Where they have an element of truth, that is twisted and distorted to make it mean something much worse than it actually is.

Over time, I have developed new beliefs. Here are a few:

1. If someone else can do it, I can learn it.

2. The more you give, the more you get.

3. I am perfect. Some of the things I do are excellent, some are OK, and the rest are the growing edges where I have the opportunity to improve.

4. There are no mistakes, only learning opportunities.

I got to where I am now through my own efforts, over many years. You can do the same. However, you can shorten the journey by having a few sessions with a good psychologist. I don't know your financial circumstances, but spending the money could be the best investment your parents will ever make in your future.

And consider me your grandfather.

Bob

To my delight, I got the following reply:

Dear Dr. Bob,

I would just like to say thank you soo much for ur help and feelings toward me. You made my birthday soo much better and more meaningful. I was feeling down on my birthday adn just got your reply the day after. I want to say I am soo glad you responded because I feel that my depression has worsened since I first experienced it. I was feeling at an all time low. I had even devoted my soul to the devil and was on the verge of practicing satanism. You really helped and I am in the process of repenting to God right now and getting my life on track. Today is the start of a new me. Thx! Bob

Tom

Naturally, I dashed off an immediate reply, though I didn't copy his spelling.

Tom, the Devil is an invention: a personification of evil acts by people. We're all children of God, with free will. God isn't an old puppeteer sitting on a cloud, but the principle of Love in your heart that you need to develop, and that's the purpose of your life. Even the most evil acts are done by people who could do differently if they only knew they had the choice.

Do an experiment. Go out and find some little kindness you can do, then keep it a secret. It can be as little as picking up a bit of rubbish on the street and putting it in a bin. The point of keeping it a secret is that a good deed is its own reward. Someone else's appreciation or gratitude is a reward, and that gets in the way.

Note how you feel when you deliberately and self-aware do a secret good deed.

This is the Jewish custom of Mitzvah. I do my best to find at least one Mitzvah to do a day. When I do it, I say "Mitzvah!" in my mind, or even aloud.

Bob

Our correspondence went on for years, and petered out when Tom went to college, and found a sweetheart. He was very proud when he qualified for a Karate black belt.

The reason I have reproduced it here is that the therapist's answers could not possibly have been written by someone still at risk of depression. The words are from a place of inner, deep contentment and self-respect. How did I get there? And how did I know I'd arrived?

My first book was published, fruit of several years of work. The publisher had organized a series of media interviews, and I was raring to go, feeling on the top of the world.

In the shower, a melody came into my mind, and I sang it at the top of my voice (out of tune, but no one could hear me). Something was odd. For the previous 22 years, that tune had signaled depression in a

1:1 association. If I thought of the tune, I'd crash. If I crashed for some other reason, the tune would start within my head. But here I was, singing it, and staying happy.

That's when I knew that after two years of self-therapy and twenty years of merely being able to control depression, I was actually free of it.

Before we go on, here is a note about a disagreement I have with every expert in positive psychology, and probably with most other people. All the way back to Aristotle, they all talk about happiness. I prefer contentment. Happiness is when my current feeling of wellbeing is above what's normal for me; unhappiness when it's below that. However, I can be currently unhappy or dissatisfied, and yet be content with life.

So, in all the recommendations below, I am offering you tools for long term contentment, regardless of moment-to-moment fluctuations in happiness.

Contentment is a skill you can learn, and improve with practice.

Let's examine key aspects of the life of someone who used to suffer from depression.

Not Happiness Ever After

Life varies; mood varies with it. When there are losses or disappointments, it's legitimate to grieve. You won't glow with joy when things go wrong. Expect to be down if you catch the flu, because the immune system uses heaps of energy, so you can't be your vibrant new self for now. When you see others suffer, it's appropriate to feel sad on their behalf. And it's OK to be sad occasionally, for no particular reason. Everyone has ups and downs. Change is the only constant, and this, too, shall pass.

Still, such realistic sources of low mood will be interlaced with good times. Their nature depends on, well, your nature. After years of carrying around the habits of depression, you mightn't become the life-of-the-party, ebullient extravert. If you do, great. But it's also fine to revel in the quiet joys of an introvert.

Remember the concept of hedonic adaptation (p 44)? Regardless of our circumstances, we tend to revert to much the same level of contentment. That may sound like doom: are we destined to stay in the pits?

No, because the level of hedonic adaptation can move. This was shown by Sonja Lyuobomisky, who also reviewed lots of research by others. She demonstrated that what people do influences their long term wellbeing. Remember, Socrates said, "Seem the man you wish to be."

For 20 years, I was OK, most of the time. A trigger would come along, and I'd crash. Then, I used a few of the tools I've outlined above to climb out of the pit again—until the next crash.

Without realizing it, however, during this time I was also doing many of the things that lift long term mood, as shown by later research into positive psychology. This time, rather than reinventing the wheel, I invented it before others, without knowing that there was such a thing. My little changes added up, and it'll be my joy if they do the same for you.

I am still an introvert; a loner by choice. My conversation is fine if I have something to talk about: it's information, not lubrication. I enjoy beauty, laugh at jokes, love children, whom I see as human puppies. Because I want a future for them, and a future worth living in, I'm a passionate environmental and humanitarian activist, and a Professional Grandfather.

I end up on the committee of every group I join, and revel in the fact that, wherever I go, people value my help and advice. In my one remaining paying activity, I am as much a teacher as an editor, doing my best to give more value than the money I receive. Everything I do is aimed at transforming a global culture of greed and conflict into one of compassion and cooperation, for two reasons: it's a better world to live in, and it's the path to survival for all complex life on earth. This gives me meaning and purpose, which in turn makes life worthwhile, whatever happens to me personally. I follow Mother Teresa's advice to help one person at a time, and to choose the one nearest to me.

I get a lot of pleasure out of physical exercise, though it's a mere shadow of what I could do ten years ago. And writing is the chocolate icing on the cake of life.

As a depressed young fellow, I compulsively helped others, as a distraction from my own woes, and I guess to try to buy affection and belonging. Now, I am of service to others, the only reason being that it gives me satisfaction. The more you give, the more you get. Decades ago, I replaced thoughts like "Oh, I wish I was dead!" with a different kind: "It's OK if I die tonight, and it's OK if I live another twenty years. It's how well, not how long." I'd still be happy not to be a human, on this crazy planet, being forced to witness all the suffering, but this is compassion for others, not sadness for myself.

OK, let's examine the tools that will take you to your equivalent, which will be different from mine in its details.

Don't Like Your World? Change it

Daniel is a builder by training, and ran his own business until 18 months before he saw me. He then decided he needed more money, and found a job with a large company that erected high-rise buildings. Dan's job was to supervise ongoing projects.

On the surface, he had it all: a loving wife, two delightful children, an income of $250,000 a year, high status in the community, the respect of the workers under him. All the same, he saw his doctor because of a long list of complaints. He'd lost a lot of weight, complained of tightness in his chest, suffered digestive upset. He really missed having time with his family. He wanted to extend his house, but simply couldn't spare the time. He used to do martial arts, rode a bike, but no longer. His job took up 60 to 70 hours a week; he barely had time to recover from work during the little time left to him.

The doctor told him he was depressed, prescribed an antidepressant, and sent him to me.

Dan explained that although he worked such long hours, he was still always behind. His typical load was to supervise thirty projects, often well apart. He needed to ensure that everything went right, sort out conflicts, prevent problems before they occurred, discipline staff... I could see him tensing up as he told me about his work.

"Can you go part time?"

"No! I wish! It's full commitment or out."

"And what are the consequences of getting out?"

"In a word, money. No way can I earn this much if I work for myself."

I decided to tell him a story from my life.

In 1978, I was in his position, with a very high-paying job that required my commitment 24/7. The job itself was great, but it left no time or emotional energy for anything else. Also, my wife and I were committed conservationists, and we figured that our lifestyle was damaging the future our children would inherit. We couldn't reduce this damage while I was working so much, because money replaced time and other activities. And as a first approximation, every dollar you spend steals from the future. (I explain this in "How to change the world," https://tinyurl.com/bobrich09 Yes, I know I mentioned it before, but it does describe a major route to contentment.)

So, at 35 years of age, I "retired." To the amazement and even ridicule of most people who knew me, I gave it all away and instead started building a house with my own hands, not by hiring Experts to do it.

As a result, we stumbled into contentment. We have raised three wonderful people into competent adulthood, while living well below the official poverty level.

I then asked Dan, "Do you have a mortgage on your house?"

"No, paid that off."

"OK, any other major debts?"

He did own an expensive car. "I could trade down, though, and wouldn't miss it," he said, not really to me.

He turned up for the second appointment, but only to thank me. He said, "I've talked it over with Helen, then gave notice. I'll be working for a builder mate as a chippie. It's a quarter of the income, but I already feel fifteen years younger. Thanks, Bob."

Not all of us can do this. You may have a huge mortgage you can't get out of, or rent you can barely afford. There may be other ways you have locked yourself into a situation in which you need to earn, or face disaster. However, reengineering your life is still possible.

All of us have needs and wants. A need is something you can't do without in your circumstances. When one of our children had her second teeth growing in a very undesirable way, she required oral surgery followed by braces. The cost was $2500. We found ways of earning the extra money, because the health of our children was a need, not a want.

A want is something you enjoy having, but if you don't get it, you won't suffer actual deprivation. If you live in a place with poor or nonexistent public transport, having a car may be a need. Moving closer to public transport can convert it into a want.

However, owning a new car, or a status brand, is a want. Having a house to live in is a need for most people in western societies. Owning a big, imposing, expensive house is a want.

I once heard the CEO of a large bank being interviewed on radio, at the time of his retirement. He started as a boy Friday in a branch of the bank, trained to become a teller, then an accountant, then branch manager, and worked his way up to the top job. His first car was an old bomb he bought for next to nothing. He stripped it down and rebuilt it. His last car was a luxury limousine. Guess which was his favorite car over all his life? The old bomb of course. When he married, they managed a deposit on a ramshackle little cottage, but then had no money for furniture. They made do. Now, he had a mansion in an expensive area.

He told us that his son had just got married. He wants a house exactly like mom and dad's. No, not the ramshackle cottage, but the mansion.

The CEO said, poor boy is missing out on the struggle, the joy of achievement. He is confusing want with need.

In my novel, *The Travels of First Horse*, my little hero said to the King of Tyre: "Majesty, why do people want more than they need? I feel that if each person could be satisfied to fill his belly and clothe his back, to have a house against the weather and beauty about him, then all this strife and unhappiness would be unnecessary."

This shedding of wants has been a huge part of my healing.

Remember, I've said that consumer society is built on necessary, continuous dissatisfaction? Opt out of wanting, and you've opted out of this insanity. One of my ongoing joys is to look at advertisements for almost anything, and think, *No, I don't want this.*

Homework

Do read my essay "How to change the world" at https://tinyurl.com/bobrich09

Engage in brainstorming with your family, separating wants from needs, and reduce the wants as far as possible. This can be a gradual process, and there is no need for heroics. It'll help you to read the transcript of a speech I made in 2002, http://mudsmith.net/yarravalley.html

Processing Trauma

On p. 38, I explained that all adult "mental disorders" are based on childhood traumatic experiences, as seen from the child's point of view. For clients like Giles, Cyril and Raelene, the relevant event was not something an outsider might identify as trauma, but it's the kid's perception that matters. An event, or an ongoing situation, induces the child to develop damaging ways of seeing the world, which then color everything.

There is effective therapy for processing traumatic experiences. It has many versions. All have a high success rate—if the activity is taken to its conclusion. However, especially at the start, doing so is scary, and even overwhelming. So, overall failure rate is high, because people start, then drop out. This often traumatizes them further.

Suppose you've had severe, worsening pain for years. An operation will relieve it, but that means going into hospital, being cut open, the pain, discomfort and inconvenience of perhaps months of recovery. That's also scary, but people do it. As I am writing this, I am recovering from a total hip replacement. It's not fun, but I know the benefits are worth it.

The same is true for "exposure therapy," the way to deal with past trauma.

It's perfectly possible to do it for yourself. A taxi driver came to me under a "victims of crime" program. One night, he picked up two men who gave him an address. When they arrived, it was a dark, lonely spot. They severely assaulted him and took all the money.

He was too badly injured to drive. All the same, the next day, on the way home from his medical appointment, he got his wife to drive him to the location of the assault. He sat there in the car for about an hour. He kept reliving the terrible event in his mind, over and over. He didn't know that he was doing the well-researched, effective therapy of "in vivo exposure" (exposure therapy "in real life").

At his first appointment a week later, he could tell me about the crime without any emotional reaction, as if it had happened to someone else. He was keen to return to work, and was actively problem-solving on ways of reducing the probability of another assault. He didn't need my services, having done therapy for himself.

The worst event of my childhood was when four bigger boys smeared feces on my face, trying to get it into my mouth. Until I was 22, I had flashbacks to this incident, dropping back into disgust, helplessness, terror. I developed a way of stopping the recall by mentally shouting, *SHUT UP!* This is a standard cognitive-behavioral technique called "thought stopping." I didn't cover it in the chapter on CBT, because it's actually counterproductive. Sure, it stopped the immediate distress, but kept the trauma going.

As a psychology student, I volunteered to do palliative care. During the training, the instructor got us to form small groups, and each of us had to disclose an unpleasant past event. When it was my turn, somehow I blurted out this memory, the first time I'd told anyone. I felt my face flame. My guts tied into a knot, and I wanted to run out of the building. To my surprise and relief, the three ladies in my group reacted with loving compassion. One gave me a hug. I calmed down.

I'd learned about exposure therapy not long before, and realized that this was what I'd just done. So, when I went home, I relaxed my body, told myself I was safe, then deliberately went back in my mind to being a little boy, in the clutches of those boys. In imagination, I saw, heard, smelt and felt it all.

I rated my distress. As you know, that's a distancing technique, moving from emotion toward reason. It was 9/10.

I deliberately relaxed again, and repeated. After the third time, the distress was 3/10. I didn't feel the need for another pass.

Since then, I've been able to think about that terrible event, disclose it as I have here, without emotional involvement. There was one exception. In Colleen McCollough's novel, *Tim*, a nasty person gives the young protagonist a "sausage sandwich:" two bits of bread with feces in between. I had a flashback, and nearly vomited.

So, what did I do? I repeated exposure therapy for my feces trauma. After two passes, my distress was 0/10. All the same, I didn't return to reading the book.

Any kind of exposure therapy is much easier with a trained helper. But, alone or with a therapist, you do the work, and once you start, you need to get through the initial high level of distress to the point where there is no distress at all. The trauma has been processed.

One way of making this technique less challenging is to start with a comparatively mild unpleasant experience, not necessarily the one you need to process. Tony was a policeman, referred by Victoria Police's health service. He'd been diagnosed with PTSD, not for any one event, but for the cumulative effects of hundreds of terrible situations.

When I described exposure therapy to him, he said, "No way. I'm scared to go to sleep because of the nightmares. I pass a spot where I had to fish a mangled body out of a car, and I'm ready to chuck up. No way am I INVITING memories like that!"

I asked if he had memories of any events not related to his work, which had been distressing, but less so. He came up with one: when his daughter was three, she'd caught her finger in a slamming door. Tony had held her on his lap, crying inside, while the doctor worked on the poor little finger.

We used my favorite exposure therapy: "age regression hypnosis." I talked him into a trance, then got him to become an eagle. He flew back to this event, changed into himself-now, and watched his younger self with love and sympathy. I got him to describe what he saw, then to rate his distress. The first time, it was 7/10, the second time 3, then 0. Seeing it work so well, he was then willing to do it on that fatal car smash, with equal success.

You can do it this way for yourself.

There are other tricks. If even having your present self as the witness to the past event is too challenging, you can see and hear it on a TV. You are your current age, in your safe place, watching the old terrible event as it unfolds like a TV show.

Once you have processed the worst traumas of your past, you'll probably find that other, less distressing events will also have lost their effect on you. You'll have become stronger, more resilient, less emotionally reactive, and more compassionate to others. Doing this is an essential step toward a life of meaning and contentment.

Homework

I recommend that you find a person with relevant expertise to be your guide in processing trauma. One option is someone certified to practice "Traumatic Incident Reduction" (www.tir.org). Another is a psychologist trained in hypnosis, EMDR, or other evidence-supported forms of exposure therapy.

As I did, you CAN do it for yourself, but if you do, ensure that you repeat the recall often enough to reduce the level of distress to trivial.

Loving the Inner Monster

Sean, an Australian Aborigine, was one of the worst-traumatized people of my counseling career. He suffered from "Dissociative Identity Disorder," that is, multiple personalities. He became a street kid at eight, and survived because of superior intelligence, creativity and courage. But, at 36 years of age, whenever he perceived a situation as involving a threat, his eight-year-old alter took over, and fought for survival. And a savage eight-year-old in a superbly fit, strong 36 year old body is terrifying.

He was invincible in a fight because he simply ignored injuries until he destroyed his opposition. At first, he brought other people into his sessions with me, he said for my protection. It took six sessions before he started trusting me, a white man, sufficiently that we could start real therapy.

I won't tell you all the many complicating details of our work together, just the one intervention that was his turning point. In hypnosis, I had him in a rowboat. He, adult, strong, wise Sean, was at the oars. Eight-year-old Sean sat in the back, holding a fishing rod, enjoying himself. He knew he was perfectly safe, because adult Sean was there, IN CHARGE.

Thereafter, whenever circumstances triggered the savage boy, he automatically remembered that the adult is in charge, and can keep the kid safe.

It may have been this experience that gave me a new realization about myself, but probably it had been growing for years before then. The inner voice that kept abusing me and putting me down, the monster of Narrative Therapy, was a very young voice. Oh, it sounded like adult-me talking to myself, but it wasn't.

It was a very hurting little child. He wasn't calling ME stupid and useless and unlovable. He was doing that to himself.

What do I always to with people who are hurting? I'm a healer by profession (though retired now), by preference, and even by nature. I give compassion and love, and do my best to help the person to heal.

So, why was I treating this poor little boy as a monster?

"Love the inner child" is a pop-psychology cliché—but it's based on wisdom.

During those many years of having depression under control, I could bash myself up for weeks before remembering to use my tools. But now, when that inner voice called me a stupid idiot, I remembered that this was a little kid, so I could smilingly let his shouting go. This went on for years, becoming more and more frequent, and more and more easy.

Note that this is still Narrative Therapy. Inner monster, hurting inner child—either way, the abusive comments are not my thoughts, but "externalized."

The process came to a peak in 2007, long after I'd healed myself, using this and other tools. In order to recover the memories of my childhood, I found a therapist even more senior, and we did age regression hypnosis (what I described for processing trauma).

All my life, I've had a distinct memory of being a little toddler, reaching up high to hold the finger of a man next to me. I'd thought that this, my only memory from before five years of age, was of my grandfather, who'd died before I was two.

In hypnosis, my therapist said: "Back. Back to the earliest thing you can remember in this life." (The odd ending is necessary. There are many recorded cases in which, without it, people experience a past life.)

I'm a tiny boy. I wear warm clothes, a bonnet on my head. My right arm is stretched way up, holding a man's finger. I see his trousered leg next to me. Oddly, at the same time, I'm looking down at a toddler, who is grasping the middle finger of my left hand. I am me, Bob, 2007 vintage, and my heart is filled with love and pity for this poor little tyke, knowing all the suffering ahead of him. I pick him up, and little-me Robi puts my arms around grandfather Bob's neck, and both my selves cry.

This was among my most healing experiences, ever. If you've gone to a therapist to process trauma, ask for something similar. If not, you can use guided imagery and do it for yourself:

- Ensure you're safe, comfortable, at ease.

- Relax your body and mind.

- Use your favorite guided imagery induction. (You HAVE done the homework for the Meditation chapter, right?)

- There are hundreds of ways of going back in time. In addition to the magic eagle, you can walk along a corridor with numbered doors; or ride in a train past numbered stations. If you use something like this, make it as vivid as possible, using all the sense-modalities. The numbers refer to your age. Walk through the door, or get off at the station, at the age you want to visit. Or say, "I'll be where I need to go," and walk through an imaginary door.

- Then, adult-you can give love to little-kid-you. If you've gone deep enough, you might find yourself to be both, like I did.

Homework

I've just described it, haven't I?

You Get What You Send

When you send out negatives, the Universe obliges and puts negatives into your life. When you send out positives, you get back positives. Note that I am NOT talking about health, wealth or other manifestations of good fortune. (That kind of "positive thinking" is nonsense. You won't win a lottery because you keep wishing for it.) It's not the cards you were dealt that matter, but how you play them. I have a dear friend, Rosemary, whom I've never met. Although still young, she is forced to be in a nursing home because of several very serious chronic health issues. She is confined to a wheelchair. This unfortunate set of circumstances has been her tool for growing spiritually. Insofar as her physical capabilities allow her, she spends all her time in making life a little better for those around her. She helps nursing home staff, looks after the requests of less mobile residents, reads to people, is a source of encouragement and help. If Rosemary can live a good life in her situation, she can inspire you in how to live yours.

If you've been reading thoughtfully, you might have noticed this pattern in many of my recommendations and case studies.

- Way back in the First Aid chapter, there it was under Creativity. A boring, low paid, dead-end job can be converted into one of fun and meaning by making it creative.

Martin Seligman, in his classic book, *Authentic Happiness*, gave a beautiful example. A hospital orderly has an unskilled, low-paid job: wheeling patients from A to B, and assisting nurses with physical tasks like turning bedridden patients. On a visit to a friend in hospital, Martin saw a man enter the room. He read the case notes, then pulled and inspected several pictures from a bag, one at a time, until settling on one, which he hung facing the patient. Intrigued, Martin had a chat with him. He was an orderly, who made it part of his work to select a picture he felt would be uniquely uplifting and pleasant for the individual patient.

- You'll find the same message in the last paragraph of the First Aid chapter: "My final email to the medical student said, 'My friend, you can pay me by passing the love on when it's your turn to be a teacher.'"

- Remember what I said is wrong with the romantic myth? It is a selfish attitude of "I want someone to love me." The key to a good long term relationship is "I want someone to love:" giving love, not taking love.

- Claire (p 57) transformed her life by turning "Not fair, why not me" into "Bless you for being happy."

- What sorted out the coffee storm? Mutual umbrage transformed into mutual giving.

- Giles's healing realization (p 64) was that he actually did matter, having been of service to others all his life.

- Remember Ricky, the kid for whom everything was an attack? I'd used Narrative Therapy with him: identified his problem as being due to sending out dark energy, rather than something wrong with him, or with the people of his world. I taught him to send out silver energy instead. Isn't that a perfect illustration for getting back what you send?

- This way of thinking is central to Acceptance and Commitment Therapy. Using one of a wide variety of devices such as the "funeral oration" or the "film script," you decide the kind of person you want to become, then do it. You can have a rapacious business shark become a beloved benefactor.

Homework

I'll next describe ways of improving your contentment, sense of wellbeing, acceptance of the bad and celebration of the good in your life.

Before reading on, do your best to invent a few ways of getting there. As I've said before, anything you come up with from within yourself works better than copying someone else. No need to take too much time on this, since I've given you several solid hints.

The Resilient Mindset

As I've mentioned, I am completing this book soon after a total hip replacement. To celebrate my improvement, I entered in a charity walk, and made a friend, Beryl. Please read the reason for my admiration for a little old lady at https://wp.me/p3Xihq-1eC

Briefly, it shows the power of determination. She was on the way home from rehabilitation after a terrible, multi-handicapping car smash, when she saw some calves for sale. She bought them, so that the obligation to care for them would force her to keep active. She deliberately imposed the need of caring for other living beings as a tool for recovery.

My little blog post about her encapsulates much of the message of this book.

I learned the relevant attitude, the first time I read *Man's Search for Meaning* by Viktor Frankl. Of course, by now you've read that book, so you'll know why. He was a genius at survival. In his book, there is not one word of hate, reproach or even resentment of the Nazis. There is not one word of self-pity. He survived because he set up a scientific study for himself: to work out why some people survived, while others gave up and died. Because he was being a scientist (a "participant observer"), he simply accepted whatever happened and kept going through incredible suffering and trauma.

There are other examples. Cabrini Pak studied the writings of eight men who had been prisoners of war, then built a good life for themselves. Some, for example Senator John McCain, became famous. She looked for indications of "transcendence:"

> The idea that human beings have a predisposition towards transcendence, whether in a spiritual, religious, or other sense, has been recognized in multiple domains, including the scientific (especially neuropsychology) and social science fields, like religious studies and sociology. Although transcendence is

defined in a variety of ways, the notion of a universal or near-universal human capacity to "rise above or go beyond the limits of," or "overcome" something about one's current situation, remains at the core of these formulations.

In a situation that devastated most people, these men became better, stronger, more resilient, because they were able to "rise above or go beyond the limits of" their misfortune. McCain realized that everyone had their breaking point, and he knew he'd reached his as a result of terrible torture. Yet after having been given time to rest, he was able to resist, and never stopped resisting. In the end, he concluded that one of the most important things in his life, "along with a man's family, is to make some contribution to his country."

This illustrates that when some extraordinary event occurs, such as torture, we struggle for meaning. When this fails, we fall to pieces. When it succeeds, we become stronger.

Certain prisoner of war camps during the Korean War were perhaps the worst described (except for Guantanamo Bay, but that's being kept as quiet as the authorities can make it).

One touching story is that of William Funchess. He suffered PTSD symptoms until he self-published a book about his experiences. He could sleep without nightmares after that. The book is out of print, but a blog article gives an excellent summary at https://tinyurl.com/bobrich10

This inspiring story tells about a man hundreds of POWs considered as their guardian angel: chaplain Father Emil Kapaun. He died, but to the very end, maintained his dignity, and refused to give in to mental breakdown.

A research paper by Segal and co-workers has examined what enabled people like him to keep striving, and even to have the inner strength to give to others, when everyone else only experienced despair and terror. "Whether religion, art, music, or an abiding faith in the destiny of humankind, those captives who saw beyond the pressures and the pain and the bloodshed to a higher order of functioning managed to defend themselves against collapse and to build the capacity for living beyond the barbed wire. One's mind, one's education, the ability to play a musical instrument, these are the things which assume higher value, things that captivity cannot easily erase."

As Nietzsche has famously said, "He who has a why to live can bear with almost any how."

Two of my favorite books make the same point through the

experiences of asylum seekers.

Najaf Mazari is a Hazara: an ethic group targeted for genocide by the Taliban in Afghanistan. After terrible hardships including torture, he was chosen by his family: "We may all be killed, and need one of us to continue the family line." He went on the refugee trail, which led to a sinking boat in the Coral Sea. The Australian Coast Guard rescued him—then he spent five years in a concentration camp, knowing every day that he could be sent back, making nonsense of his sufferings. He is one of the lucky ones, though, and now has a prosperous carpet business, and is a respected member of society.

His book, *The Rugmaker of Mazar-e-Sharif*, recounts these harrowing experiences, and yet will make you laugh, time and again, joining him while he gently laughs at himself. And every cent he earns through his writing supports good causes back home in Afghanistan. He has financed ambulances, and girls' schools (the toxic distortions of Islam have a particular hatred of education for women).

The second book of this kind is the life story of Para Paheer, a Tamil young man from Sri Lanka. He became a student leader, which made him a target of the authorities. After horrid torture, he and his wife escaped to India. But when the Sri Lankan civil war ended, India forcibly sent refugees back, despite validated evidence of continuing murder and torture. Leaving his wife and little son, Para got onto a people smuggler boat, which, you've guessed it, sank. The determination, decency and courage of a merchant ship captain led to the rescue of most of those on the crowded little boat, and they ended up in Australia's concentration camp on Christmas Island. Then, he was adopted as honorary son by Alison Corke, after the two managed to exchange emails. To understand why I love this book, read the title: *The Power of Good People*.

Note that being resilient doesn't stop you from suffering. The trauma still has its effects, which may include PTSD. You still need exposure therapy, or some equivalent. However, if you have meaning and purpose, you will cope, regardless.

So, when things get tough for you, see how you can help others. My walking mate, Beryl, deliberately created a need for herself to have an obligation to a bunch of calves. If you have honest belief in a religion, immerse yourself in it, and it will lift you to extraordinary heights, as it did for Father Kapaun.

Only two things matter in this life: what we take with us when we die, and what we leave behind in the hearts of others. Remember this, and you can emotionally survive the worst that ill fortune may throw at you.

Homework

If you haven't already done so, read the three books I've mentioned (*Man's Search for Meaning* by Viktor Frankl, *The Rugmaker of Mazar-e-Sharif* by Najaf Mazari, and *The power of Good People* by Para Paheer and Alison Corke), and others like *I am Malala*.

Follow these people's example, even if your circumstances are far more fortunate.

Moving Hedonic Adaptation

Sonja Lyuobomisky's work demonstrates how to move the level of "hedonic adaptation." Following her recommendations has a great benefit: it's fun. I've been doing these things for decades. Some I learned from books and courses. Others I learned from characters in the novels and short stories I've written. And there are a few I invented myself.

Here is my adaptation of Sonja's recommendations:

Focus on the positives

> A little bird went flying by.
> As I wiped it from my eye,
> I said, "Thank heavens cows don't fly."

When describing the ABC diary, I'd said, "Attention is a searchlight. Whatever it shines on stands out, while everything else recedes into background. Attention is also a fertilizer. Whatever you apply it to grows, while everything you withdraw it from withers away." Sonja's research shows that forming the habit of focusing on positives (the silver lining on the cloud) improves resilience, makes you into a more effective problem solver, and lifts your mood.

Again, though, we need to go with the golden middle. This is not a Pollyanna denial of bad things, but of coping with them by focusing on possible solutions, on ways of coping. (The bird DID plop in the poet's eye.)

Here is an example. When I'd built my house, I installed all the plumbing, then got a plumber to check the system. Twenty years later, a leak developed in a component, and I went to fix it. In the meantime, the copper pipe had got hard and much less flexible, so when it was time to reassemble, I just couldn't get the final joint to line up.

After half an hour of futile struggle, I dropped my tools, rested my head on my hands and groaned, "Oh, I can't do this!"

Relapse!

What did I do? I told myself, "I installed the bloody thing, so I can fix it." This changed my perspective. Instead of struggling with the joint, I looked at the whole situation carefully, and saw a twist in a copper pipe. I borrowed a gas blowtorch, heated the pipe to re-anneal it, then did the job in a few seconds.

Reframe the bad

Henry was given notice that he would be retrenched in six months. He was actually required to train his replacement, a man from India who'd then go home and do the work at a quarter of the cost to his employer.

He decided to get what he still could out of the company, and used their employer assistance scheme for a few sessions with me.

He'd never suffered depression before. I said he wasn't now: it was legitimate grief.

As part of therapy, at a certain stage I asked Henry to find the good things about his coming loss of a job.

He came up with: more time with family and friends; having the opportunity to study and gain a new qualification; and to convert a token vegetable garden into one that would feed them the year around. (In Melbourne, Australia, this is perfectly possible. I've done it.)

I asked if seeking another job should be on the list. He said, he'd be more flexible about time commitment by setting up as a consultant, and had already started researching how to do it.

A second example is a scientific report, just published as I write, about the recovery of wild bee species in Detroit, see https://tinyurl.com/bobrich11

This city of once two million people now has 700,000, many with low incomes. Abandoned buildings are everywhere, as are empty lots overgrown with weeds that are never sprayed with horrible poisons. So, the bees have returned.

The remaining citizens of Detroit, 80% of them African-Americans, have done wonderful silver-lining with urban farming, which they are now supplementing with honey production. That's a very sweet example of getting good out of bad.

Keep the good fresh; adapt to the bad

When bad fortune strikes, you need to problem solve, so you can reverse or at least lessen its effects. For example, if you've had a stroke, you can often significantly improve your functioning through appropriate exercise, and being determined to get better. Only giving up stops improvement. Nevertheless, you'll probably never be the same again. It's a serious loss. It will also drag you down emotionally, but if you quickly adapt to the new normal, you can return to your previous level of wellbeing. The way to do this is to establish a routine, as regular as possible. Once you are used to the new normal, you can start to grow from there. Remember Rosemary, and Beryl's recovery?

When your circumstances have improved, slow down adaptation. This is done by engaging in dynamic and intermittent activities that focus your attention on the positive change. That is, actively and repeatedly remind yourself of your good luck, but keep varying how you do it.

Send out good

The most important good thing you can send out is *metta*. What is that?

Jesus said, "You have heard that it was said, 'You shall love your neighbor and hate your enemy.' But I say to you, love your enemies and pray for those who persecute you." This does not mean that we should put up with evil, with bad or even thoughtless behavior, but that we should deal with the perpetrator in a spirit of helpfulness and compassion.

English is an imprecise language. The word "love" has five different meanings. This Love Jesus talked about has a special word in Greek: "agape," pronounced /agapi/. The conventional English spelling can result in confusion with having your mouth wide open. So, I prefer "metta," which is what the same concept is called in Buddhist writings.

You can be an atheist and practice metta, and sadly, you can claim to follow a great religion like Christianity, and do the opposite. This is not a religious concept, but an ethical one.

It is deliberately making the choice of treating all other humans as our brothers and sisters. Read the wonderful Dalai Lama's wonderful book, *How to Practise*.

For many years now, part of my daily meditation has been to send out metta. Sometimes, it's to a particular person who needs it. Sometimes it's to members of some group, like everyone in my neighborhood. It can even be to all living beings on earth. The hardest, of course, is to send it to myself, but that's what I occasionally do. Because I don't want to adapt to this activity, I vary it all the time, so it's always fresh.

It is important to note that the recipient doesn't need to know of my sending. The good effect is on me. If I also have a good influence on the other person, beauty.

Walking along a street, driving a car in traffic, sitting in a dentist's waiting room, wherever I encounter other people, I often use one of many devices to send metta:

- "Metta to you," I might think at a grumpy, aggressive-looking fellow.

- "Have a good life, you two" could be a silent wish for a young couple walking hand in hand. Wishing the other person a good life is often what I do when finishing a phone conversation with one of those pesky callers who try to trick money out of me.

- Here is a wish I often use when finishing an email, or within my mind to a stranger:

> May you live in contentment;
> May you be healthy (or "May your health improve" for someone in ill health);
> May you rise to your challenges;
> And may you grow spiritually.

- I've designed a collection of emailable cards. Each has a picture, and a wish to go with it. Here are a few of the wishes:

> May EVERY DAY of your year be:
> full of MEANING and PURPOSE
> CONTENTMENT and JOY
> BEAUTY and HARMONY.
> Every day is special.
> Cherish it, treat it as if it might be the last day of this life for you.

Another card has a picture of a huge, beautiful tree, with the text:

> May your taproot anchor you to our planet.
> May your branches reach the sky.
> May your great lateral roots stabilize you against the storms of life.
> May your being enrich the soil, purify the air, provide bounty for all that lives.
> And when you finally pass on to the next stage of your existence, beyond death, may you be a better person, thanks to having lived, this time.

Then there is a photo of a beautiful eagle:

> Her mighty wings lift her on the thermal updraft, lazily circling, far above all pain, all worry, all grief.
> If she chose to flap those wings, she could fly with great speed, to any place, any time.
> She is a magic eagle.
> The great feathers of her tail steer her wherever she wants to go.
> Great fierce beak; great fierce claws: everyone respects an eagle.
> Up there she soars, perfect for her world, and her world perfect for her: Queen of the Sky.
> Be that bird.

You're welcome to use my words, but it's more fun to make up your own. Find a nice pic to go with each, but keep file size small, and honor copyright.

Sonja's work, and my personal experience, show that it's essential to keep varying everything about sending metta, as is the case for all the devices I am describing below. Remember, we are actively raising long term mood, and this is done through variety, freshness, creativity, humor.

People are made happy by accumulating experiences rather than possessions

If you've read my essay "How to change the world," you'll know that I agree with Sonja. Note my self-control: I didn't include the link again.

Wealth, status, power over others, fame and the like are trinkets.

I've discussed this before. Meeting challenges; growing in skills, wisdom, maturity and spirituality lead to contentment.

You might become a world champion. Then you have the incredible, anxiety-provoking struggle of staying there. But long after you've retired, you'll still have the wonderful memories.

I suspect your achievements will be somewhat less notable than being a world champion. That's OK. For example, I've never been a great rock climber, but under supervision I once completed a famous, quite difficult traverse: the "Three Sisters" in Katoomba, within the Blue Mountains of Australia. That's a good memory, and it doesn't matter if it makes me better than anyone else, or if it's a trivial achievement compared to what someone else can do.

Tolerance

The Qur'an states that Allah is the only judge. Muslims who attack others for apostasy, for breaking Mohammed's injunctions, are as wrong as judgmental Christians.

I don't know from which nation, but there is a Native American saying: "Do not judge me until you have walked in my moccasins for 100 days."

A great deal of unhappiness comes from blaming. Deliberately let it all go, insofar as you can. You don't need to be perfect.

A bunch of young men used to rent a house near me. They sometimes had noisy parties, with music I find unpleasant. Several neighbors were very upset, and eventually managed to get the authorities to evict the boys. My solution? I had a pair of earmuffs next to my bed. If a party started, I slept with them on. Besides, being skilled in mindfulness meditation helps.

Forgiveness

Forgiveness and tolerance go together, but are different. Say this wonderful Buddhist prayer, aloud or within your mind, once a day:

> If I have caused harm to any being, knowingly or unknowingly, accidentally or on purpose, then I ask for forgiveness.
> If anyone has caused me harm, knowingly or unknowingly, accidentally or on purpose, then I offer forgiveness.

It needs to be taken seriously, from your heart. The best time is when settling for sleep, because "you could possibly die during the night, and you should leave no bad feeling behind."

Be of benefit

The *mitzvah* is a beautiful Jewish custom. It is a secret good deed, which need not be anything major. When you do it, say "Mitzvah!" within your mind.

Here are a few recent examples from me. (Mind you, they've stopped being mitzvahs, because I've let other people know about them.)

- I've picked up a sharp-pointed screw from a bike path, saving an unknown cyclist from a puncture.

- I saw a poor little beetle on its back, desperately waving its legs in the air. I turned it the right way up. Since I'm sure its level of understanding is not sufficient to have it appreciate the deliberate kindness, I counted it as a mitzvah.

- Similarly, I fished a spider out of a half-full bucket of water.

- A lady was posting a letter. It fell out of the slot of the letter box as she walked away. Making sure no one noticed, I picked it up, and posted it for her.

- As I was driving along, I saw that the car in the next lane would soon be stopped by an illegally parked car. Being as unobtrusive as I could, I hung back, so the driver could change lanes.

Why should the mitzvah stay a secret?

In Jewish ethics, an act is its own reward or punishment. Suppose I steal something, and am never found out. My punishment is that God and I both know that I am a thief. (In Buddhist thinking, it's a debit on my karma. According to Muslim beliefs, an angel sitting on my left shoulder writes it down, and it'll be evidence against me on the Day of Judgment.)

If I do a good deed, my reward is that God and I both know that I'm a good person. (Or it's a credit on my karma, or the angel on my right shoulder writes it down.)

You can be an atheist and appreciate the logic.

Suppose my good deed is public rather than a secret. Then, I get extrinsic rewards: another person's gratitude, admiration or appreciation. "Thank you" is sufficient reward, so I can't also claim the inherent one of becoming a better person.

Besides, it's more fun that way.

Gratitude

Sonja's book cites lots of evidence on the benefits of gratitude, in any set of circumstances. She recommends making a daily gratitude list, something I've been doing every now and then for years. (Naughty: I don't remember it every day.)

Before my first hip replacement, I experienced severe chronic pain, all the time. One night as I settled for sleep, I thought, *Great! Today the pain never went above 7/10!*

I've heard my wife say something wise when someone commiserated with her about getting old: "It's an honor and a privilege: an achievement."

When you're in a good situation, regular gratitude keeps it fresh and effective in keeping you contented. When you're in a bad situation, finding things to be grateful for is a good way of focusing the searchlight of attention where it is needed.

Understanding

The evidence shows an apparent paradox here. If you work at understanding and explaining positive experiences, they become predicable and ordinary. This speeds adaptation, which is the opposite of what you want. Simply accept your good fortune with gratitude.

Doing your best to understand negative experiences leads to acceptance. For example, writing about past trauma helps to resolve it. Thousands of people have made sense of their suffering by writing a book about it. I've edited many like that. However, if you choose this path, note that a book can do one of two things, but not both. Either it's a form of exposure therapy that helps you to heal, or it's helpful for others, providing a service to help them to avoid or overcome suffering. If you want to do both, do so in separate books. This is because we're all unique and different, and a sample of one can never suit a large group of others. Naturally, you can have autobiographical bits in a helping book like I'm doing here, but only after you've resolved your own trauma.

Homework

Every day, even every instant that you remember, do something that will help move your long term mood.

You don't need to stick with the above list, but rather use it as a guide. Adopt those practices that seem most natural, and use them, though always in a varied way. Over time, switch to others, or add more techniques to your daily list.

Using these recommendations as a template, make up your own. Always, the tool you invent is more powerful.

Celebrate yourself whenever you do any of these things.

I use a mixture of deliberate rituals and intuitive, occasional flashes of action.

Flow

As a boy, I found two antidepressants that worked for me.

One was study/reading. Fiction took me out of my world, out of my life, into excitement, adventure, the ways of thinking and being of other people. I lived in places I was sure I'd never visit in real life, became the people I was reading about, and while entertaining myself, I unknowingly started my apprenticeship as a psychotherapist.

In a way, nonfiction was even more satisfying. Laugh if you like, but I loved to read encyclopedias, starting at A and working right through. History, geography, geology, astronomy, if it taught me something, I was hooked. While my mind was fully invested in all this fount of knowledge, I could forget about being an unlovable, ugly klutz. Hours passed without me realizing it, and sometimes I accidentally missed a meal because I was caught up in, say, theories about the formation of the universe, or the way differential calculus works.

This state, this kind of involvement, is what Mihály Csikszentmihályi termed "flow" in his classic book of that title.

My second antidepressant was running. First you warm up, then get into a smooth rhythm. After a while things start hurting, you're puffing for air, and it takes effort to keep going. But... when you push through this pain barrier, you're in heaven. You're fully functional in the real world. For example, you keep safe from road traffic, adapt to going up and down hills, handle tactics and strategy if it's a race. You may be monitoring yourself on a stopwatch. Nevertheless, within your being, time stops. There is no thought, no emotion, no hurt, just a smooth flow of being. I called this state "being in the zone," and got thoroughly addicted to it. For years, I trained three hours a day, covering 100 miles per week—which is why I now have two artificial hips.

I don't advocate this level of involvement in anything. The golden middle is better: too much is as bad as too little. But then, I no longer need to run away from being myself.

By the way, I doubt you can achieve flow while running or walking with one of those things in your ear, blasting you with music. That's a distraction. You need to BE the activity.

Mihály writes, "The best moments usually occur when a person's body or mind is stretched to its limits in a voluntary effort to accomplish something difficult and worthwhile." His best example is a young man who worked on an assembly line, something most people find soul-destroying. Look up Charlie Chaplin doing it at https://tinyurl.com/bobrich12

For this young man, however, it was forever-fun. He achieved this by converting his job into almost an Olympic-level sport. His task was supposed to need 43 seconds. His best at the time of Mihály's study was 28 seconds, which he tried to beat, hundreds of times a day. This was, he said, more enjoyable than watching television. Think about it: a basketball player will practice hundreds of penalty shots, a pianist goes over and over the scales, a swimmer may spend hours perfecting the tumble turn. This young fellow was doing the same.

I read Mihály's book in 1990, when it first came out. In preparation for writing this chapter, I've read it again, and am surprised and gratified by the bits I've forgotten. He says many of the things I've told you so far. For example, his work empirically demonstrates that "symbols" of happiness like wealth, fame, power, physical beauty actually have nothing to do with wellbeing. "The quality of life does not depend directly on what others think of us or on what we own. The bottom line is, rather, how we feel about ourselves... To improve life one must improve the quality of experience."

An essential component of flow is a match between the challenge of a situation and your skills in meeting that challenge. You're bored if what you do is too easy, and find the situation overwhelming if it's too hard. If you enjoy an occasional social game of chess, playing against a grandmaster will make you feel stupid and helpless, and bore the grandmaster out of his mind, unless he chooses to adopt a teaching role. Fun, a pleasant challenge, is to play against someone a little better than you. Also, that's the way to improve your skills, so playing chess can become a lifetime source of enjoyment and mental growth.

However, it's easy to spoil this. If you play the game for its own sake, as a pleasant challenge, you're having fun whether you win or lose. A chess world champion said, "You learn far more from games you've lost than those you've won." But if your focus is entirely on winning or losing, then you've sacrificed the inherent value of the activity. A win leads to gloating, a loss to despair and anger. There is no fun in that.

When I was playing a competitive chess game, in a sense I stopped existing. There was nothing but the position in front of me, calculations of possibilities, an eye on the clock, often reactions to the known personality and playing style of my opponent. At the end of a session (completed game, or adjournment after 40 moves), I was exhausted, my knees shaking, with hardly the energy for the trip home. And this was immensely satisfying.

One warning is that, in the way running was for me, flow can become addictive. As Sonja has shown, you need constant variety and change. Getting stuck in the one thing, however pleasurable, is counter-productive from the perspective of gaining long term contentment. You need to work toward complexity, variety, meaning. Sure, a few people with exceptional potential can become world-beaters in a particular activity like tennis, or cooking, or playing the violin, or revolutionizing a field of science. That doesn't necessarily make them feel content. In any case, Mihály says, it's better to "become a dilettante—in the finest sense of the word" in many areas; to develop sufficient skills to find delight from many sources, both mental and physical.

Mihály quotes Bertrand Russell when describing the kind of personality who can feel satisfaction in life: "Gradually, I learned to be indifferent to myself and my deficiencies; I came to center my attention increasingly upon external objects: the state of the world, various branches of knowledge, individuals for whom I felt affection."

Note the progression. The great philosopher wasn't always like this. He built this personality for himself. You can follow him.

Mihály's book, *Flow*, is above all a thought-provoking, fascinating read. It is as much an exploration of philosophy as a recipe for an enjoyable life. It is worth reading in its own right, regardless of what you may learn from it.

Homework

Read *Flow* by Mihály Csikszentmihályi, and use the regular activities of your everyday life in the way I used running and reading as a boy; the way that young man performed his factory work. For those still in the grip of depression, flow gives holidays from misery. For those who already enjoy long periods of contentment, it's a tool for living far above the "normal."

<table>
<tr><td>**7**</td><td></td></tr>
</table>

Spiritual Care

My Greatest Teacher

His name was Siddhartha Gautama. Over 2500 years ago, he established a great philosophy, which many people mistake for a religion. However, you can benefit from his teaching and stay a Jew, or a Hindu, or a Christian, or an atheist. The Qur'an explicitly contradicts some of the Buddha's teachings—but then, the Bible, which Islam accepts as Allah's word, implies the sun moving in the sky above an immobile earth. (That's why Galileo was persecuted.) So, you can keep your current belief system, and gain from this chapter. You merely need to accept the validity of a few scientific findings, and adopt ways of thinking that may be new to you.

You can be a "secular Buddhist:" follow the teachings without practicing any ritual. That's what I've done all my life.

There is a remarkable similarity in the therapeutic applications of Buddhist thought and modern psychology; e.g., the Dalai Lama has written several books that recommend actions just like some of what I've covered above. His book, *The Art of Happiness*, ranks with Seligman's *Authentic Happiness* and Csikszentmihályi's *Flow* as one of the standards of positive psychology.

In relatively recent times, therapeutic practice has moved explicitly toward a Buddhist-inspired direction. Several approaches, like ACT, are mindfulness-based, and there are many other overlaps.

Buddhism differs from any religion in that that the Buddha told us never to accept anything on someone else's authority, but to check it out experimentally, through personal experience, something like, "This has worked for me. See if it works for you." If it doesn't, there is every chance that you can use the idea to invent a method for yourself that will work for your unique makeup and situation.

I won't give you a primer on Buddhism. If you're interested, there are many sources of information, based on each of the several versions of this wonderful belief system. However, here are a couple of important points.

Time Is An Illusion

The past is history. The future is a mystery. I give you a PRESENT. (Pity this only works in English.) Look at a river. Glance away, and look back within a split second. It seems the same, but the water has moved. It is actually different.

A problem with our European-based culture is that it's caught up in the past and future. We tend to beat ourselves up because of past events, and worry about things that may or may not happen. Mark Twain said, "I've had a lot of worries in my life, most of which never happened." There are hundreds of quotes saying this. One I like is from Shannon Alder: "The true definition of mental illness is when the majority of your time is spent in the past or future, but rarely living in the realism of NOW."

You might enjoy "Buddhism for Christians" https://tinyurl.com/bobrich13 (a discussion I've had with a Christian gentleman). It is one of four relevant essays at my blog, the others being "I is a Paradox" https://tinyurl.com/bobrich14 "Vipassana Appraisal" https://tinyurl.com/bobrich15 and "Second Vipassana Appraisal" https://tinyurl.com/bobrich17

Noble Truths

The second point is the source of all the negatives, and what to do about it. This is the heart of Buddhism: the four "Noble Truths." The first three are important for understanding what I describe below. The relevant terms have no English equivalent, but this is a reasonable approximation:

"All life is suffering. All suffering is from attachment. So, to stop suffering, let go of attachment."

Let's expand this.

The Buddha didn't imply that life is continuous misery with no relief, but that even good times tend to have underlying niggles. Nirvana is whenever these disappear, not only from consciousness, but even from the stream of unacknowledged thought and feeling below it.

Because only this instant exists, nirvana is only for now.

Attachment is when I want something. If I dislike any aspect of my current moment, I want it to go away. If I like something, I want it to continue indefinitely, and am anxious about losing it. This second aspect is why even good times are suffering. "Oh, I want this to last forever" is a recipe for disappointment. Nothing does.

So, the way to enjoy the good things is to enjoy them now, but not be attached to having them beyond this instant. And the way to be content despite the negatives is to allow them, and not be worried about their continuation. I have a standard joke for this situation, say being late for an appointment because the train is behind timetable: "It's probably not fatal, and even if it is, that's all right."

When you can let go of attachment, suffering stops, and you're in nirvana. If you can achieve this as an ongoing state, you are enlightened.

I'll discuss two aspects of Buddhism I have found useful in moving toward a life of contentment, regardless of my circumstances. Follow these, and you can feel OK in hell.

Reincarnation

I will now demonstrate that reincarnation occurs. I will show that it is no more a matter of belief than, say, the adaptive value of sickle-cell anemia. For millions of people, me included, it is based on personal experience. As I've described in *Ascending Spiral*, in 2007 I recovered memories from five past lives. More recently, I exchanged hypnotic past life regression with a colleague in Scotland, via video conferencing. She recovered a couple of past lives, and so did I. However, going through the exercise, I heard a voice that was not a voice, but a thought that was not my thought: "It is only spending time." This told me that the lives I recalled in 2007 were the only ones I needed to know, in order to do my work in this life.

Why is reincarnation a wonderful tool for achieving contentment?

Because it allows us to learn from experience, to progress in spiritual development, to gain from suffering. This is why I titled my story "ascending spiral." We go up and down, forward and back, but over a lifetime, most people grow and improve in some ways. Extend that for many lives, with lessons from one life influencing others, and you have inevitable overall growth. I make sense of our world by considering us to be caterpillars feeding on the green leaves of experience, until at last we graduate into butterflies. That is the state of enlightenment, when we can get off the wheel of life. It is when we have learned all the Lessons we can learn, the final one being metta, the one from Jesus, of unconditional, universal love for all.

I'll explore the implications for living after reviewing some of the evidence.

The Evidence for Reincarnation

Buddhist beliefs contain a genuine paradox about reincarnation. Because all is One, there is nothing separate that can be born again, that continues beyond death. In fact, the entire material universe, including human bodies, is an illusion, so also, there is nothing to reincarnate into. Several versions of Buddhism are very strident about this. At the same time, if you die with unresolved issues, you're required to return into a new life in order to resolve them. Other Buddhist writings take this for granted.

In my essay, "Buddhism for Christians," I describe the wave analogy that explains this. Do read it. Here, instead, I'll look at the scientific evidence concerning reincarnation.

Can there be scientific evidence for such a concept?

Yes. First we need to examine what "scientific evidence" means.

There is no proof in science.

I have a hunch about something. To test this hunch, I try to DISPROVE it. I set up a way of gathering information that has a chance of showing my guess to be wrong. In science, this is called the null hypothesis.

If my procedures reject the null hypothesis, then my hunch is supported.

I am not perfect, and my preconceptions could have biased my results. So, there is need for others to be able to repeat my study, perhaps with some variations. If they agree with me, that's cross-validation. My hunch is now a theory.

From that theory, we need to make further predictions, different from the original one. We try to disprove these too. If we can't, then the theory is supported. This is "converging evidence." The more unrelated, different lines of evidence support the theory, the stronger it is.

OK, on that basis, there is strong scientific support for reincarnation. Two examples below will meet the strictest standards. Another one is "hearsay:" people's opinions, which is inherently not scientific evidence, but adds support to the other two. (This includes me telling you that I've had past life recalls, without objective, confirmable evidence. However strongly and honestly I believe what I say, it could be my imagination, or wishful thinking.)

Hypnotic Past Life Regression

Check out the work of Peter Ramster: https://tinyurl.com/bobrich18

Peter was a psychologist in Sydney, Australia, who found that some of his hypnotic subjects slipped into past lives (most hypnotists find this, me included). He did something new: got the person to make testable claims. For example, one woman felt herself to be a male medical student a long time ago, and drew the interior layout of the medical school in Glasgow, Scotland.

Peter got a research grant. He took four such clients to Europe to check each of the four claims.

They found that the Glasgow medical school building had an entirely different layout. But... a local historian had old blueprints of the building, before extensive renovations. They EXACTLY matched the drawings the woman had made in Sydney. No one had looked at those old blueprints for many years.

Two of the other three cases were also exact matches. The fourth had slight inaccuracies, but was substantially correct.

Given that in the hypnotic trance this lady felt being a man who had this knowledge, I can't think of any other explanation than that she'd lived as a medical student in Glasgow, before the building's renovation.

Children's Past Life Recalls

The best known investigation into past lives is that of a team at the University of Virginia, that's been examining testable "odd" claims by children under seven years of age since the 1950s. Their website is http://www.uvadops.org/

Ian Stevenson was the first Director of the institute, and wrote many books about their research. Given the skepticism of western culture regarding reincarnation, he and his colleagues were super-conservative in their conclusions, and meticulous with their research techniques. In 2002, he retired, and Jim Tucker took over his role. Jim's personal website http://www.jimbtucker.com/ lists all their publications, and is a fascinating place to visit.

The technique is to seek out little children who know things they should have no way of knowing, or can do things they shouldn't be able to. For example, consider a three year old boy who keeps saying he is Bobby Jones the golfer, has a fascination with golf although his family has zero interest in the sport, and as he grows, he becomes a junior champion with a string of 22 wins in junior golfing contests. This is one of the cases in Jim's second book, *Return to Life*.

The investigators interview the family, and get the child to make testable claims regarding which the family doesn't have relevant knowledge. They then go looking for the evidence.

Jim's first book, *Life Before Life,* is an absorbing read. When he wrote it, the team had 2500 cases in which, despite every attempt to explain the findings as being due to other causes, only one conclusion was possible: this child had lived a previous life.

As well as giving an overview of the research and its findings, Jim discusses 25 cases in detail. Some of these are reprints of articles in high reputation scholarly journals.

In preparation for writing this section, I lashed out and bought Jim's second book, *Return to Life.* It is chattier, is in fact autobiographical, and is convincingly honest. When a case has doubtful features, he states them. It is less "scientific" and contains more speculation, perhaps because western culture has moved on and is more accepting of the possibility of reincarnation.

Chapter 4 is particularly convincing: a little boy with many verified memories of having been a pilot, shot down in the battle of Iwo Jima. I won't repeat the details, but it is simply impossible to account for the story in any way apart from reincarnation. Similarly, Chapter 5 is a great detective story, in which we read the progression of the case, all Jim's caveats and doubts—and the overall conclusion that little Ryan had to have been a person in Hollywood in the 1940s.

Return to Life is like a detective game. Jim presents evidence, and lets you draw your own conclusions about a case. He then discusses deeper issues: how are reincarnation and similar observations compatible with science? This part is 100% relevant to the reason I am covering reincarnation here. There is a side trip into an excellent common-language explanation of quantum physics, which I also find fascinating, and the detour is well worth it, even if physics is foreign country to you. Basically, modern physics demonstrates that the physical reality we feel around us is the creation of consciousness. This then makes sense of findings showing that there is an ongoing, nonmaterial part of a person that can move from life to life. The final conclusion is that all is One, and we apparent individuals are components of a Consciousness.

I thoroughly recommend reading either of these books.

Clinical Death and Out-of-Body Reports

One of my clients was a young woman who'd had many major operations. She told me that while anesthetized, she usually found herself looking at the hospital from outside. On occasion, she'd looked in through a window, watching them working on her body.

Another lady had died from pneumonia, but was revived. She has an unshakeable memory of sitting on a log near a creek in a forest clearing, with her long-dead grandfather comfortingly sitting beside her.

In the Preface to her book, *Ortho-Bionomy: A path to self-care*, Luann Overmeyer gives a vivid, very believable account of dying in a motorbike accident. She saw her body in the ambulance while her consciousness was above the vehicle. While she hadn't been able to see auras previously, now each person wore a glow. She watched from up near the ceiling as her body was left alone in a room. One nurse walked in—and looked up at Luann. She told her to go back into her body. Luann did, and lived to become an expert in a field of healing.

There are thousands of such accounts. The most beautiful is by Yvonne Rowan, which was her contribution to my book on cancer. She has given me permission to reproduce it here:

Yvonne's story

I was not afraid to die, having already done it once. When I was 26, I bled to death, the result of a miscarriage. There had been simply a painless drifting away as nurses frantically cut off my clothes and covered me with dripping towels, and a panicked voice: "Open your eyes, Yvonne! Wake up!... Open... your..." faded to black.

Some time later, I became aware of no longer being in my body, a literal sense of release—no longer a prisoner in the flesh, sentenced to hell on Earth. I had lived in a state of shock. Life stunned me with its injustices, its pain, its cruelties. Fate, like a malicious wind, buffeted me through a meaningless life, deprived of purpose. Often I stumbled through my days on automatic pilot, while inside I huddled in a fetal position in a deep, dark corner, collecting mental and emotional dust; and the ghost of Poe's raven drove me ever deeper with his whispers, "Never good enough. Never good enough." I wondered if we would still mourn for our dead if we knew death was the end of a prison sentence—and suicide an attempt to escape.

Suddenly, I had been set free.

And there came a dazzling light and an unyielding sense of peace and love. A tunnel of light revealed the way to eternity, and I knew that if I could reach the brilliant light at the end of that tunnel unnoticed, I could stay. Propelled by a mere thought, I raced toward my goal.

A voice that was not a voice commanded, "Halt!" And the

word made it so. Halfway to eternity I stuck, unable to move.

"You must go back. It is not your time." The Voice was gentle, loving, but firm.

I resisted, arguing with (God?) in vain. "I don't want to go back," I dared to defy.

"You must go back. You have not yet completed your purpose there."

"Purpose? There is no purpose. I don't want to go back."

"Your children need you."

"Someone else will raise them, and do a far better job than I can. They'll have a better life without me to mess them up."

"They need *you*. They were not given into your care by accident."

The thought roused me slightly from my despair, my apathy. Instinctively, on some level, I knew this Voice could not lie; it could speak only truth. Its truth appalled me.

"What insanity is this?" I demanded. "Because it was insanity to give four children to ME to raise! And I'm doing it alone—*all* alone!"

"They need you. And there are others who need you, others you don't know."

"In case you haven't noticed, I can't even take care of myself. My life is one major disaster. I don't want to go back to it."

The Voice relentlessly exuded patience and love. "You have no choice. You must complete your purpose."

"Someone else can do that, too."

"No. Only you can do it. You were created especially to fulfill this purpose."

"Purpose, purpose. I have no purpose. I'm nobody special. Anyone can do what I do, and do it better."

"You alone have the specific qualities necessary to fulfill your purpose. No one else can do it."

Suddenly scenes appeared before me like a holographic movie. I watched, fascinated by the revelation.

And then the Voice again: "If you do not go back, it will not be done."

Horrified, I relented and was immediately sucked back into my body.

* * *

My life did not instantly improve, although I was forever changed by my "near-death" experience. Crisis was home to stay, it seemed, but my attitude, my view of life traveled at a new altitude. Mostly, anyway.

New understandings and certainties settled in and cuddled up to crisis, easing the pain, smoothing out anxiety, comforting my fears. I no longer feared death: I had seen the other side. This is *not* all there is. Death is an illusion. In fact, I felt more like I was being born than encountering death—and suddenly I had a new perception of Christ's admonition about the need to be born again before we could enter 'heaven'. It made sense to me as it never had before. Birth in a physical body was required in order to enter the physical world; so, too, was birth in a spiritual body required to enter a spiritual world! *I wasn't dying*, I thought. *I was being born!* But it was "not my time," I was told; there is a right time for everything.

As a direct result of my experience, I also absorbed a different view of 'accidents' and 'coincidences'. Are those words we use when we can't see the whole picture, the connections? And speaking of words, what power they have! The Voice said, "Halt!" and it was so. God said, "Let there be light... and worlds... and creatures..." and it was so. And thoughts: I had a thought, and action followed. Thoughts have energy, power; they make things happen. I understood, and became much more careful and mindful of what I thought and said.

But I did not understand the most important thing of all, and I became obsessed with it. I now knew undeniably that I had a purpose, a specific purpose that must be fulfilled before I would be allowed to move on. Eager to get on with it, I tried to remember what that mission was. I remembered vividly every detail of my time on the other side, except that. I tried hypnosis and meditation. I read. I reasoned. I thought. I strained. But those holographic scenes had been wiped from my memory with an indelible eraser. It seemed that nothing could retrieve them.

Soon it became the only thing I thought about, the only thing I prayed about. I asked my Higher Power; I cried; I pleaded; I cajoled—and when my frustration nose-dived into anger, I raged.

"How can you do this? You give me a mission, tell me it's vital, claim only I can fulfill it—yet you *refuse* to let me remember it! Well, I refuse to be held responsible if it goes unfulfilled! I *refuse to be responsible!* Do you hear me? How can you hold someone responsible for something you won't even let them know? How *dare* you! How *dare* you call yourself fair and just!"

And one day, in the midst of my raging, a voice that was not my voice slid quietly into my mind. Had I not recognized it, I possibly would have immediately committed myself into the nearest "safe" place where medication was considered part of the daily diet.

"Do you see the bee?" it asked gently.

"Huh?"

"Do you see the bee?"

"What does a bee have to do with this?" I felt more than a little belligerent.

"What purpose does the bee serve?" so softly, lovingly, the Voice prodded.

I considered the question, not willing to shut off communication now that it finally was happening. "I suppose you could say it feeds the world. If it didn't pollinate the plants, all life would cease—or at least all of it on land."

"Do you suppose the bee is aware of its purpose?"

I smirked. "No, I seriously doubt that it has given it a single conscious thought."

"And yet it fulfills its purpose splendidly simply by being what it was created to be, wouldn't you say?"

"Yeah, I guess it does."

"And so it is with you."

Silently I contemplated this concept, without wanting to accept it.

"All things have a purpose essential to the whole. If any would fail, all would fall. Each fulfills its purpose by simply being what it is. Conscious awareness isn't necessary... Besides, knowing mankind as you do, what do you suppose would happen if each of you knew your specific purpose?"

"Ah, that's easy. We'd insist on doing it our way instead of Your way and undoubtedly screw it up!"

"So stop worrying about it and just be the best *you* that you can be."

I took that advice, and the sense of failure that plagued me became meaningless, while my life took on a focus that carried me through the crises fate continued to plunge onto my path.

Twenty years later I again found myself on my deathbed.

Now I remembered these things and was not afraid. I knew I was dying—again. My family and friends knew I was dying. Soon. We were by now resigned to it.

Pervasive weakness conquered the last remnants of strength, and I could barely lift my hand. Agonizing pain gripped me relentlessly, but at least the violent vomiting and nausea had abated. A heart attack followed too closely by acute gall bladder and liver disease had left me within days of death.

So, I thought, *my purpose was finally fulfilled. Mission accomplished.* Perhaps now I would find out what it had been.

Listlessly I looked at my mother standing in the dim room next to my bed. Her steel-gray hair was tousled. Tears oozed from her clear blue eyes and coursed down her pale, smooth cheeks.

"Are your affairs in order?" Her soft voice tried too hard to be steady. "Are there any arrangements you need to make?"

I had made no arrangements for anything. I hadn't planned on dying, and it was too late now. I hadn't the strength to even think about it, never mind get out of bed to see a lawyer about writing a will, or making funeral plans.

"No," I answered.

My granddaughter, Jericka, stood next to her: the joy of my life, the one I lived for. I'd raised her from the day she was born. My daughter had been a mere child at her birth and was now lost in her own hell into which I could not reach. Jericka and I had become as close as any two people could be. We could read one another without words—she, peering over the edge of pubescence, breasts straining to bud, promising eventual full-bloom, full life—and I, life-weary and worn beyond willingness.

I stared at the jelly-jar glass stuffed with the dandelion bouquet she had brought me earlier, and remembered another day, the day she had taught me about dandelions.

Was it last spring or the spring before? We walked along our road, flanked by Picasso-splashes of spring flower colors. Jericka was enthralled by their abundance, needing to know the names of each one—"What kind is this, Nana? And that one? And, ooh, that purple one over there, what's it called?"—burying her nose in some to absorb the sweet fragrances.

We came to a field carpeted in eye-shattering yellow. "I want a yard just like that," she declared, "with lots and lots of dande-lions." When I told her most people consider them to be weeds, she scoffed. "How could people think such a beautiful flower could be a weed!"

Gently plucking a fully blooming dandelion with one hand and a lollipop of fluffy seed with the other, she studied them intently for a moment before wanting to know how one became the other. Satisfied with my brief explanation, Jericka-the-imp, with her sideways grin and flirting eyes, blew the seed into my hair. "You look like the baby chicks!" We laughed: Our chicks were molting and looked like harassed little cartoon warriors with their cottony down poking out in every direction...

...I would miss her—her honest simplicity, her fresh view of life. I looked into her Van-Dyke brown eyes, fringed with thick black lashes.

She knows, I thought. I could see it in her face. *She didn't believe it until now... but now she knows I'm dying.*

I've never seen anyone look so lost. Eight years old and wondering, "What will happen to me? Where will I go when you're gone, Nana? Who will love me then?" She spoke not a word with her mouth, but every fear, every question, every pain was written clearly in those soul-deep eyes and trembling lips.

Her anguish pinched my heart, eclipsing my own pain. My love for her filled my soul, and an irresistible yearning replaced my resignation. I prayed.

"Dear God, You know I'm not afraid to die. But I love this child so much. She needs me. She has no one else who will care for her like I do. To the world I may be a weed, but to her I'm a dandelion—a dandelion with a vital mission. Surely I'm not yet finished here, am I? Please, for her... let me live."

I used to work in the medical field, so I know how much difference the will to live can make, and the importance of something to live for. I wonder, though, how often we confuse the will to live with feeling worthy to live.

Life still stuns me with its dark side.

But I live, with purpose—and I am not afraid.

* * *

Jericka is grown now. Yvonne and I still exchange the occasional loving email. I put it to her that the reason she had to return from her first death was so she could choose to return to suffering the second time, for the love of a child. This hadn't occurred to her, and she agreed.

The trouble with such accounts from the scientific point of view is that they are unverifiable. However believable an account may be, it's only someone's honest opinion, and we humans are excellent at fooling ourselves.

Actually, Jim Tucker has cited several reports in which a person in this state made a verified claim. For example, one person unconscious on the operating table reported being out of body, and seeing his mother smoke a cigarette in the waiting room. That was the first cigarette of this middle-aged lady's life, and was completely unexpected and therefore unpredictable.

Some people have spent a long time in a coma, perhaps kept alive by machines. They tell a story of being in contact with Someone, who doesn't judge them, but requires them to relive their life from the end toward birth, experiencing the effect they've had on other people. When the effect was positive, the experience is strongly motivational for building on their strengths. When it was negative, the person will learn from it, and typically wants to make restitution.

This is the meaning of *karma*, which is not reward or punishment, but learning from past lessons like this, and setting up opportunities for the lessons the person chooses. This was my personal experience during my past life recalls.

Incidentally, you don't need to die to deal with karma. I once acted negligently, and as a result a calf got terribly hurt. For years, I bore the guilt, and was sure I'd need to return as a calf to pay for this act. But a wise person asked, "What has been the effect on you?"

"I've been very careful since to avoid injury to any other animal."

She explained, "You've learned this lesson, so you won't need to learn it again."

What is "Between Lives?"

In *Life After Death*, Deepak Chopra claims that beliefs in this life shape what we experience immediately after death. Australian newspaper tycoon, Kerry Packer, had a clinical death experience, and stated that there was nothing but darkness. What's the bet he was an atheist, and believed that there is nothing beyond a material existence? Jim Tucker has studied claims about what things are like between lives, as reported by a considerable number of the children his team had investigated. The accounts are extremely variable, and strongly culture-based. For example, many from western cultures see a glow, while those from Asia tend not to. So, this is indicative evidence for Deepak Chopra's description.

Deepak goes on to say, though, that after a while (whatever that means, since there is no time in the "other place,") this illusion goes, and the processing of karma occurs, led by a Guide, in the way I described for myself.

On the Buddhist view, life is an illusion. This entire material universe is. We are kept in this illusion, and required to keep returning to it, by hanging onto certain ways of thinking and being, which presents us with issues demanding resolution; the sources of suffering. On this view, processing karma, and setting up lessons for the next life, makes perfect sense.

This issue is the reason Jim Tucker's *Return to Life* includes an extensive exploration of quantum mechanics. The conclusion of modern physics bears out the Buddhist belief that the material universe is a projection of Consciousness. What is, is "life energy," which creates matter and energy by observing it. This sounds bizarre, being stated like this, but read any account of quantum mechanics and you'll be forced to this conclusion. Max Planck, one of the originators of quantum mechanics, said, "I regard consciousness as fundamental. I regard matter as derivative from consciousness. We cannot get behind consciousness. Everything that we talk about, everything that we regard as existing, postulates consciousness."

Reincarnation and Suicide

Someone asked the His Holiness, the 14th Dalai Lama, what was the greatest regret of his life. He said, an old monk once came to him, asking to study a particular Buddhist discipline. The Dalai Lama gently explained that this needed to be started at seven years of age. In his current life, the old man couldn't possibly do it. So, the man killed himself, presumably in the hope of being able to take the relevant path in the next life.

This cannot work. Suicide was such a debit on the man's karma that after death, he was certain to require restitution for the act in the next life. Being denied the opportunity for learning this discipline is the only possible restitution.

The same goes for suicide for any reason, or no rational reason at all. It's a way of running away, probably from the very lesson situations the person was born for. As with the processing of trauma, running away from it only prolongs it. Suicide never works to solve problems, only to have them repeat.

Summary

I have described two lines of evidence that give excellent scientific support for the existence of reincarnation. I haven't read the studies about verified out of body experiences, but that's probably a third line of support. If I were a defendant in a court of law, and my case depended on having the validity of reincarnation accepted, this evidence would be considered to prove it.

Implications for Living

Life has inherent purpose. This is not the accumulation of wealth, power over others, or fame. It isn't happiness or contentment. We are here in order to learn Lessons, life after life, progressing toward perfection. Those who reach that can get off the wheel of life. And since even the last life is a learning experience, we don't need to live perfect, only to die perfect.

Several versions of Buddhism emphasize that "there is a Bodhisattva in everyone." No matter what you have done in the past, there is a chance for you to achieve enlightenment, in this life.

Yes, this means you. (As I write, that little voice inside me says, "Yes, Bob, your readers, but of course not you!" I smilingly send him metta, and ignore his opinion.)

Suffering is the spur to growth. Some of your suffering may well be restitution you've chosen for misdeeds or mistakes in past lives. Others may be your chosen lessons. You can identify them because your nose keeps being rubbed in the same lesson, time and again. This may be major, but can also be a small matter. Remember, on p. 59, I talked about using clarifying questions with myself in order to minimize inappropriate reactions? When I do this, it works for me, but I keep forgetting. Often, I open my big mouth and needlessly hurt someone. Then new information comes in, and I have to bear the guilt of disobeying my own philosophy. ("Above all, do no harm. If you can, do good. If you can't do good, change the situation until you can.")

I'm in exactly this situation, right now. I bought something on eBay, and never received it. I made a complaint, and implied dishonesty on the vendor's part. After several messages via eBay's complaint system, my wife suggested where the item could have gone. I won't go into the details, but she was right. The item WAS delivered, and had I done some detective-style thinking a few days after the due date, I could have avoided hurting another person.

Obviously, this is something I need to be mindful of in the future. When I have learned this Lesson, I'll have become a better person.

Not everything negative is a karmic load. But whatever the reason for bad fortune, it gives you an opportunity to grow. Also, the bad fortune of another person gives you an opportunity to be helpful and compassionate, and that is the most important step toward enlightenment.

Homework

Visit and watch the series of videos about Peter Ramster's work at https://tinyurl.com/bobrich19

Read one or both of Jim Tucker's books, *Life Before Life* and *Return to Life*.

Regardless of whether you accept reincarnation as true or not, work on these questions: "Suppose it's true. What are my chosen life lessons? How have I reacted to them in the past, and how will I do so the next time I have the opportunity?"

Equanimity

Dealing with severe physical or emotional pain

I've said previously, my major reason for bouts of sadness is for the coming environmental catastrophe that will kill billions of humans and other creatures, and probably result in the extinction of all complex life on earth. I am a professional grandfather: love children and want them to have a good life, knowing they won't.

The tool I use every day, for this issue and for a great many lesser ones, is "equanimity" or acceptance. I've left it till last, because it's the most powerful tool there is.

Jon Kabatt-Zinn's technique for coping with severe, chronic physical pain is to calmly observe it, and allow it to be there. This works just as well for emotional pain. The following page has a card entitled "Acceptance" that I used to give to my clients.

OK, so I am told that a friend has just had a baby. I get the instant pain of knowing that this new person will grow older in a world of horror. That horror is active, right now, in other parts of earth, but we in the so-far lucky places are due for it, soon. So, I drop into advance grieving for this child.

Then I remember: the past is history, the future a mystery; I give you a PRESENT. I may be wrong (wouldn't that be wonderful!) and the horror may never come. Besides, my thought is only real if I buy into it. It's a thought, and an emotional reaction to the thought. If I can simply accept the thought, acknowledge its presence, allow it to be there, then the suffering goes, and I can smilingly congratulate the parents.

Acceptance

Geniuses at survival can live in hell, with peace in their hearts. We can learn from them. If I don't like something, I need to work at changing it. But that takes time, and may never succeed. For now, I can simply accept it. Best illustration is pain.

Pain = sensation + emotion.

1. I have an unpleasant sensation. If I simply accept it, I'm not hurting. It can stay there, I'm OK.

2. Sometimes I can't manage this. Then I'm hurting. I can accept that for now I'm hurting, in pain, do want it to go away—and it's OK to feel like that. Then I may be in pain, but it's OK.

3. Sometimes, I can't do this, and am in despair: "What's the point of living like this?" If I can accept that for now, I'm in despair, I can still carry on.

Acceptance at one level may allow return to a better one, but can't be done for that reason—or it's not real acceptance and won't work.

If on a particular occasion I can't get rid of the pain, then I can acknowledge that I feel it, and it's OK to feel it. I can feel the pain, and share the parents' joy at the same time.

And if I have really slipped into the black hole of anticipatory grief for this tiny newcomer, then I can accept that. I can still put a smile on my face, one of genuine metta, and congratulate the new parents.

It's even worse, of course, when I think of my own loved ones. And yet, perhaps 90% of the time, I am fine. I do live a life of contentment. When I slip, I simply accept that, for now, I have slipped, and this, too, shall pass. It does, and I slip up into contentment again. It's not a race, not a performance I need to measure or struggle with. What is, is, for now.

Writing fiction is one of my joys, one way I can enter the state of "flow." (Mind you, I'm in flow right now, as I write.) A huge benefit is the people I invent. I learn from them all the time.

Bill Sutcliffe is one of my teachers. He is the "Doom Healer," whose task is to eliminate all evil on Earth. The hero of a science fiction series, right now he only exists in my computer, but I'll publish his story one day. In the meantime, he helps to keep me sane in a crazy world. As a fifteen year old boy, he made a speech that featured on the world stage. Here is an extract:

In preparation for today, I studied past talks here, and wrote a similar speech. Like the others, it's full of information, dense— and boring. I've posted that speech to my website, with references, and will instead just talk to you. My excuse is, after all, I'm only a kid.

First we need to deal with the horror of what's coming. As George said, climate change will kill billions. We're past the tipping points.

We arrogant humans have looked on this planet as the only seat of intelligent life. It isn't. Merlin, the alien the recent solar flare killed, told me there are millions of locations of intelligent life within our galaxy alone, and there are innumerable galaxies. All those places, including Earth, are schools for souls. The body dies, but the life energy of an animal or a plant continues. There is sound scientific evidence for reincarnation.

So, those billions will return, if not here, then to some other school within the universe. This is because we have a job to do. Merlin told me, we need to live again and again, learning and advancing, until we have evolved sufficiently. You're not here to become wealthy, or famous, or powerful. You're here on a journey toward becoming like Jesus, like the Buddha. This is not a matter of religion. You can be an atheist, but if you attain a life dedicated to Love, what we call by the Buddhist term metta, then you qualify for Buddhahood.

Everything ever born must die. We can die one at a time, or billions together. That doesn't matter. We can die before birth, or 100 years old. That doesn't matter. Even suffering is only short term. In the long view, we can shrug that off. All that matters is progress along the journey toward moral perfection.

I hope I've eased your pain.

You can read the document on his website at https://tinyurl.com/bobrich20

It actually isn't boring. People who have read it responded with compliments (to me, not to Bill, because they don't understand that reality lives in my computer).

Does equanimity always work? Bill Sutcliffe taught me another story about that: "This Buddhist abbot was famous for his equanimity. Then robbers attacked the monastery, and were slaughtering his monks. He kept screaming and crying. His deputy said, 'But Father, what about equanimity?' The abbot answered, 'Equanimity is all very well, but they're KILLING MY PEOPLE'!"

If even the abbot could forget the deepest level of equanimity, then us lesser-trained mortals can be excused when we do so. You don't need to be perfect, only to do your best.

Dealing with Success and Failure

This logic can be applied to absolutely anything. Suppose you are training for a contest. Sonja Lyuobomisky's research shows that you'll get the most emotional benefit out of the total experience by aiming for the sky before the event, but accepting whatever the outcome is, once it is over. This is equanimity.

Similarly, she says, when something positive happens in your life, smilingly accept it with gratitude, but have minimal expectations for its benefit. That way, you're less likely to be disappointed, and more likely to get a pleasant surprise. When there is a negative change, simply accept it, seek solutions, but accept frustration if these attempts are unsuccessful. Strive to do the best you can, and be content with the outcome.

Homework

Especially if you have severe, chronic pain, but even if you don't, get hold of Jon Kabat-Zinn's two-CD set, *Mindfulness Meditation for Pain Relief*. You'll find it beautiful. Apply it to the worst pain (emotional or physical) in your current situation.

By now, you should be highly skilled at detecting all the thoughts and automatic reactions that drag you down. Accept them with equanimity instead of buying into them.

8 Depression in the Family

When I have finished a book, I seek feedback from "beta readers." Fellow inspirational writer Jennifer Bonn suggested, "I wonder if you would consider a section with maybe how to have a conversation about depression with the family... how the family can help."

So, here it is. And this chapter is well worth reading even if you are not in this situation.

Suppose you're OK, but someone you love is tortured by depression. What can you do to help?

Healing can only come from inside. However frustrating it may be, you cannot "fix" someone else. Part of depression is feeling hopeless. "The world is a terrible place, and is guaranteed to continue that way forever. What's the point of doing anything anyway?" No amount of argument, encouragement or guidance will shift this view, because it isn't based on reason. People cannot just "snap out of it."

All "mental disorders" have this kind of irrationality. The starkest example is when an anorexic, skeletal person looks in a mirror and sees fat.

You may have noted how this applies to depression in the many case studies I've described. However, these people came to me as clients: seeking help from a stranger. I could work with them precisely because I was a stranger. When members of my family suffered from some devastating event, all I could do was to give them a loving hug, be there for them, let them tell me anything without judgment or advice, let them say nothing if that was what they needed to do at the time.

Not only could I not do therapy with relatives or even friends, it actually would have been unethical for me to do so. That is termed a "dual relationship," and is a no-no for a reason. You're sure to share the emotions of people you care for. You cannot lead someone out of an emotion by joining in.

Here are two examples of how I achieved "professional distance" when needed.

I once had a "victim of crime" client: a blind old gentleman whom a bunch of teenagers bashed up. They also hurt his old seeing-eye dog. I visited him at home. When I left, I worried that I wouldn't be able to work with him, because my sense of outrage got in the way of the professional relationship. So, that evening I started what I thought would become a short story in which a far worse criminal teenager would get just retribution. This is the standard technique of "displacing emotion." I invented two people: a fourteen year old boy who murdered six little kids and a woman, and an old lady, Sylvia, who was the witness. Only, Sylvia then took charge, and the story became one of the power of compassion. It grew into a novel, *Hit and* Run, which many of my fans   have   considered   as   my   best. http://bobswriting.com/hitandrun.html

Twenty years earlier, my daughter fell from a horse, and suffered multiple fractures of her right arm. I splinted the injury to reduce her pain, and make the ride to hospital bearable. I achieved professional distance by repeatedly saying inside, "It's only a broken thing I need to fix." I collapsed a second after handing her over to the professionals.

Normally, however, you don't want emotional distance from your family; rather, the opposite. Nevertheless, there are things you can do when there is depression in the family (or somewhat further away, like a friend).

Caring for the Carer

You must first look after your own welfare. The first lesson of nursing is, "You can't care for others until you care for the carer first." The second lesson is, "It's not your pain; you're not there to share it but to relieve it." In a therapeutic relationship, "professional distance" is one step further: you are not even there to relieve the pain, but to guide the sufferer to do so.

How do you ensure that your loved one's misery doesn't drag you down?

Um... read the book again:

- Put the seven recommendations of my first aid chapter in place: healthy eating, adequate sleep, regular vigorous exercise, regular fun, creativity, social connectedness, and meaning.

- Learn to relax your body, and do so whenever unwanted muscular tension intrudes on your awareness.

- Meditate daily, and in odd moments when you have the chance. This should include both mindfulness and guided imagery meditation (not at the same time, unless you're a lot better at it than I am).

- The strongest, most powerful tool is equanimity/acceptance. That applies to any problem. Read that chapter again.

- You may feel some guilt, especially if the person struggling with depression is your child. By all means, examine if any past or current action of yours may have contributed to the problem, but responsibility is one thing; guilt another.

Dealing with Guilt

Suppose you've identified some way you have contributed to the fact that your child is now depressed.

I'm sure you did the best you could at the time, and no one can do better than that. Here is a card about this:

Mistakes

There is no such thing as a mistake, fault or defect.
There are only learning opportunities.
When you make a mistake:
1. Apologize to yourself within your heart, and forgive yourself.
2. If possible and appropriate, apologize to other people affected.
3. If possible and appropriate, make restitution.
4. Work out how you can do it better next time.

If you find that a past act was a mistake, that's proof that you've gained in wisdom.

The worst thing you can do is to beat yourself up with shame and guilt. You're responsible for having made the mistake, and the above addresses that.

Homework

You may never have been depressed. All the same, reading the preceding chapters will improve your life. You might even enjoy the journey! If you have already done so, continue using the tools that lead to contentment, because they help you to rise far above "normal."

Inducing change and growth

The Healing Relationship

Carl Rogers was the first person to systematically apply the scientific method to psychotherapy. His work established that inner growth is facilitated when a person is in a certain, very special social situation: with someone who reacts with "empathy, genuineness, and unconditional positive regard."

Empathy

This word has entered common language, but it's worth a brief discussion. It isn't sympathy (feeling sorry for), but more like "I appreciate where you're coming from." When someone shows empathy for me, I feel understood, accepted, valued.

However, this is not "I know how you feel," but more like "I can see you're suffering and am here for you."

Unconditional Positive Regard

Rogers didn't want to use "love," because of its multiple meanings, particularly the romantic/sexual one. He meant what I have called metta. "Whatever you have done, whatever you may do in the future, I deeply and honestly care for your welfare." Metta doesn't excuse bad behavior, but responds with love anyway.

When my son was a toddler, he sometimes refused to obey until he got a little smack on the (well-padded) bottom. This wasn't physical punishment, since it didn't cause pain, but more an attention grabber. Invariably, about five minutes later, he'd climb onto my lap to show he "forgave me." An age-appropriate version of this is what we need. For example, you might say to a teenager, "However much I love you, I won't accept you speaking to me in that tone of voice."

Genuineness

People pick up false metta, and false empathy. Pretense won't work.

How to use this in helping others

The Dalai Lama has written that the reason we should work at becoming enlightened is that this enables us to be of service to others.

When intuitively, automatically, without effort, you always react to everyone with the Rogerian virtues, you have become enlightened. Heaven knows, I am not there yet: I often react to people with negative emotions. However, every such situation is a training opportunity. I need to ACT as if I were enlightened, and genuinely treat people with empathy and metta. And yes, this is perfectly possible. It needs a suitable reminder, such as "I need to reject the action, but accept the person."

When you do this, you become an agent for change. Most people, though of course not all, will react to you as a rainbow in their lives.

You will succeed in this on some occasions, not at other times. That's fine. Apprentice Buddhas don't yet need to be perfect, and knowingly or unknowingly, all of us are apprentice Buddhas. Celebrate your successes, and accept your slipbacks with equanimity.

Also, you're allowed to be human. Perfection is so boring!

Homework
Remember the three Rogerian virtues of empathy, genuineness and metta. Practice them with everyone, as far as you can. You only need to do the best you can, in this instant.

The Power of Showing
A huge body of research indicates that a youngster can achieve enormous changes by deciding to imitate an admired role model. As a teenager, I had the benefit of copying several wonderful adults I think of as my "angels." I can now be your guide because I decided to be like these people.

I wrote a short story demonstrating the power of modeling for an earlier draft of this book, but my publisher wants me to keep word count below 50,000. So, you'll find it at my blog: *Armour-coating our kids*. The link is https://tinyurl.com/bobrich21

In *Hit and Run*, Sylvia transformed the young multiple murderer simply by being herself. Despite all his abuse, her reaction was to help with his concern for his little brother, who was the only person he loved. She was the first adult, ever, who'd treated him with respect and caring, so he decided to become like her, at first only with language (because she'd convinced him that this enabled him to get his way). Through the many twists of the story, he found an increasing number of positive role models.

Research shows this works even for drug abusing, alcoholic, violent kids from the slums, so it'll work for your child, who doubtless has far fewer problems.

So, back to the previous section. Act in the way you would like your child to be as an adult. There is no need for explanations and lectures, but you can use a little trick.

When making changes, you need to pick on one identifiable habit at a time.

> "Michelle, darling, I decided to do something very difficult and need your help."
>
> "Uh, what?"
>
> "You know how I sometimes shout at you kids when you break family rules?"
>
> She pulls a face. "Yeah, I've noticed."
>
> "From now on, I'll do my best to speak calmly but firmly, correcting your behavior, but with love. When I manage it, I want you to notice, and show your appreciation. And when I fail, and go back to the old way, I'd like you to simply say, "Hey mom, you're shouting again."

This does many things:

- Gives power to the child, which is especially useful for someone struggling with depression.

- It's actually extremely useful for you in achieving your habit change.

- It's highly likely to provide her with a role model to copy.

- It breaks an ongoing negative cycle, transforming a source of conflict into one of cooperation.

- When she corrects you, I have no doubt that both of you will burst out laughing.

- Finally, it is highly likely to improve the kids' behavior.

Helping an adult

Nina was the receptionist at a high-power business. One day, after she'd done a conscientious job of helping a middle-aged customer, he said, "Miss, I wouldn't want to be married to you!" He had a twinkle in his eyes, though, so she decided not to take this comment at face value.

"I'm devastated," she answered with a smile. "What have I done to deserve a rejection?"

"You're so nice at work, you just HAVE TO crash and be a grumpy harridan at home."

Sure, this is funny, but it's based on truth. Many people struggling with depression do exactly that. Have you noticed, often we're at our worst when we feel safe? I used to lecture to hundreds of students, train tutors and run tutorials of my own, and nobody would have guessed the empty space I felt myself to be. When I got home, I could crawl into a hole and pull it in after myself.

Someone who bleeds behind the happy mask may acknowledge the depression, or may be in denial. If your loved one is the first kind, help is available. Eight to twenty sessions with a good psychologist, or a conscientious application of my program here, can enable this person to make lifelong changes. You may have to insist, and be forceful about it, like Shirley was with Giles (p. 39), though tough love doesn't need to go to the extent of ending the relationship. "I'm here for you, whatever happens, whatever you do, but I hope you realize that your depression is causing me misery, too. For my sake, see a psychologist."

Denial is much harder to deal with. As usual, argument, the presentation of facts, is unlikely to work.

First, you need to protect yourself. For this, the "assertive formula" is ideal:

Assertive Communication

You can handle an annoyance in three ways:

1. Bulldozer: "Get off my toes or I'll punch your face in!"

2. Doormat: "Sorry for being in your way. Please trample on me."

3. Assertive: "You're standing on my toes and it hurts. Please get off now."

The assertive formula is: "When you do this, I feel... so please do that."

You don't need the formula in words, but use the philosophy behind it.

So: "Darling, I'm alone at home with the baby all day. When you come home and hide behind your computer, I feel like a single mom. Talk to me. Tell me about your day, take an interest in mine."

"Susie, sorry, I just don't have the energy!"

"I think it's more than that. When was the last time you had a good laugh, at home not at work?"

Don't push too hard, but plant seeds for thought. He isn't doing this to cause harm, but because he is suffering. Empathy and metta go a long way. Requesting couple therapy can work. In the presence of a professional, you can state your opinion that your partner is depressed, and list the evidence.

Positive psychology can also be very helpful.

Jacob often came home to find the breakfast dishes still in the sink, bed unmade. Since Carol had lost her job, she spent all day sitting in front of the TV with a blank look. She once actually asked, "Oh, did you forget something?"

"No. It's late afternoon and I'm home from work."

"Oh."

She, however, denied that there was anything wrong. "I'm just a little tired, that's all."

He couldn't get her to see a psychologist, so came to me himself. I did second hand therapy with her, by teaching him many positive psychology techniques like the list in Part 5, particularly those that involve being of service to others. He then practiced them himself, quite ostentatiously. She did get intrigued, and tried out a few. To her own surprise, she found herself laughing on occasion, and gaining energy to become more active.

For her birthday, Jacob bought her two books: the Dalai Lama's *The Art of Happiness*, and Martin Seligman's *Authentic Happiness*.

Two weeks later, she made an appointment with me to deal with her depression.

Homework

Don't do anything immediately, whatever the age of your loved one, or the relationship between the two of you. Think about the issues, and go gently, with empathy and metta.

And small steps go a long way.

<table>
<tr><td>

9

</td><td>

Dealing with Relapse

</td></tr>
</table>

There is only this instant. Right now, you may have permanently and irreversibly freed yourself from depression. Five minutes from now, you might be in the pits again.

Here is the "relapse prevention" card I used with face to face clients when I still had them:

Relapse Prevention

Old habits always come back. The difference between a glitch and a relapse is what you say to yourself.

Relapse: Bashing yourself up. "I knew I couldn't do it. I am useless, hopeless, what's the use? I might as well be dead!"

Glitch: Forgiving yourself. "Everybody has an occasional slipback. It's OK. I've beaten it before, I can beat it again. Now, how can I prevent another glitch in the future?"

Either way, it's a self-fulfilling prophecy. Kindness to yourself, resolving to do better and learning from it maintains improvement.

```
  _ _                      _
 / \/                     / \_
```
"I can do it better."   "I am a failure."

When helping people with addictions, I got them to prepare an internal statement in case of a slipback, e.g., "I've beaten a 20 cigs a day habit for two years. I can beat a one cig once habit."

You may remember my 10-second relapse while struggling with plumbing. One positive thought allowed me to step back, and look rationally at the situation. The relapse was gone.

By conscientiously working through this book, you've achieved contentment. When you do have a glitch, simply reapply the same tools.

The best is equanimity. "I feel like crap. My despair is 7/10 for now.

That's all right." If you can truly and honestly accept that you've slipped, and it's all right, then, paradoxically, the low mood will probably go away. (Remember, though, if you "accept" it in order to have it go away, then you haven't accepted it, and it won't work.) But even if, for now, you're in the dumps, you can feel content with life, so it doesn't matter. "Who has ever said I need to be perfect?"

And as with everything, this, too, shall pass.

Even processed trauma can return to pester you. I've given an example on p. 87: I'd detoxified my memory for when four bigger boys put feces on my face, but when reading a book, I was ready to chuck up again. What did I do? Another session of exposure therapy, which could be briefer.

Finally, if you've been serious about applying this program to your life, you're now far more resilient, more able to cope with anything. You'll have far more insight into the inner workings of your mind, so you can gently laugh at the old tricks of your inner monster/child who tries to trip you up again.

You are not what you do, but the person doing it. If you happen to be doing depression again, for now, that's fine. Change is the only constant.

Apply this logic, and your bounce-back can be as soon as you like. Of course, you may want to enjoy a little misery for a while, and that's all right, too.

I hope that, after reading this little book, you consider me your friend. Email me at bob@bobswriting.com about anything.

Have a good life. Regardless of circumstances, you can.

May you live in contentment.
May you be healthy.
May you rise to your challenges.
And above all, may you grow spiritually.

References

Beck, A.T. (1967) *Depression: Clinical, experimental, and theoretical aspects*, NY: Harper & Row

Beck, A.T., Ward, C.H., Mendelson, M., Mock, J., & Erbaugh, J. (1961) An inventory for measuring depression. *Archives of General Psychiatry*, 4,561-571.

Beck, J. (2011) *Cognitive Behavior Therapy: Basics and beyond*, 2nd edition, Guilford Press

Caspi, A., Sugden, K., Moffitt, T.E., Taylor, A.E;, Craig, I. W., Harrington, H. & McClay, J. (2003) Influence of Life Stress on Depression: Moderation by a Polymorphism in the 5-HTT Gene, *Science*, 301:386-389

Chopra, D. (2008) *Life after death*, London:Rider & Co.

Csikszentmihályi, M. (1991) *Flow*, Harper Collins

Dalai Lama (1998) *The Art of Happiness*, New York:Riverhead

Dalai Lama (2002) *How to Practise: The way to a meaningful life*, London: Rider & Co.

DSM 5, Diagnostic and Statistical Manual of the American Psychiatric Association, https://www.psychiatry.org/psychiatrists/practice/dsm

Edwards, L., (2010) High achievers more likely to be bipolar, Medical Press
https://medicalxpress.com/news/2010-02-high-bipolar.html

Elkins, D.N., Robbins, B.D. & Kamens, S.R. (2012) Open letter to the American Psychiatric Association from the Society of Humanistic Psychology, a division of the American PsychAssn.
http://www.apa.org/monitor/2012/02/changes-dsm.aspx

Engdahl, B.E. & Page, W.F. (1990) *Epidemiology in military and veteran populations: Proceedings of the second biennial conference* March 7, 1990, National Academies Press

Flannery, T. (2002) *The future eaters*, Grove Press

Frankl, V. (1946, current imprint 2017) *Man's search for meaning*, Boston:Beacon Press

Garn, S.M., Bailey, S.M. & Cole, P.E. (1976) Similarities between parents and their adopted children, *Am J Phys Anthropol.* 45(3 pt. 2):539-43

Funchess, W.H. (1997) Korea POW: *A thousand days of torment, November 4, 1950-September 6, 1953,* self-published

Gathercole, M. (2004) Development and exploration of a new model for understanding depression, *Australian Journal of Counselling Psychology,* 5(4):7-17

Goodman, L., Thompson, K. & Weinfurt, K. (1999) Reliability of violent victimization and PTSD among men and women with serious mental illness. *J Trauma Stress* 12:587–599

Goldman, R.N. & Greenberg, L.S. (2015) *Case formulation in emotion-focused therapy: co-creating clinical maps for change.* Washington, DC:American Psychological Association

Greenberg, G. (2010) *Manufacturing depression: the secret history of a modern disease,* Simon & Schuster

Greenberg, L.S., Rice, L.N. & Elliott, R. (1993). *Facilitating emotional change: the moment-by-moment process.* New York:Guilford Press

Harris, R. (2007) *The happiness trap: How to stop struggling and start living: a guide to act,* Wollombi, NSW, Australia:Exisle Press

Herman, J. & Schatzow, E. (1987) Recovery and verification of childhood sexual trauma. *Psychoanal Psychol* 4:1–14

Hoopes, L.L. (2017) *Prosilience: Building your resilience for a turbulent world,* Georgia:Dara Press

ICD *10 International Statistical Classification of Diseases and Related Health Problems, 10th Revision,* WHO http://apps.who.int/classifications/icd10/browse/2016/en

Kabat-Zinn, J. (2010) *Mindfulness meditation for pain relief: Guided practices for reclaiming your body and your life,* Sounds True Publishing

Kabat-Zinn, J. (2016) *Mindfulness for beginners: Reclaiming the present moment and your life,* Sounds True Publishing

King, P. (2004) *Your Life Matters,* Random House

Klerman, G.L. & Weissman, M.M. (1989) Increasing Rates of Depression, *JAMA,* 261:2229-2235

Lyuobomisky, S. (2010) Hedonic Adaptation to Positive and Negative Experiences. Ch 11 in S. Folkman, (ed) *The Oxford Handbook of Stress, Health, and Coping,* Oxford University Press

Mayo Clinic *Persistent depressive disorder (dysthymia)* www.mayoclinic.org/diseases-conditions/persistent-depressive-disorder/symptoms-causes/syc-20350929

Mazari, N. & Hillman, R. (2011) *The rugmaker of Mazar-e-Sharif*, Melbourne, Australia:Wild Dingo Press

Melartin, T.K., Rytsälä, H.J., Leskelä, U.S., Lestelä-Mielonen, P.S., Sokero, T.P. & Isometsä, E.T. (2002) Current comorbidity of psychiatric disorders among DSM-IV major depressive disorder patients in psychiatric care in the Vantaa Depression Study, *J. Clin. Psychiatry*, 63(2):126-34

Meyer, I., Muenzenmaier, K., Cancienne, J. & Struening, E. (1996) Reliability and validity of a measure of sexual and physical abuse histories among women with serious mental illness. *Child Abuse Negl* 2:213–219.

Neeld, E.H. (1990) *Seven Choices: Taking steps to new life after losing someone you love.* New York:Bantam Doubleday Dell

Overmeyer, L. (2009) *Ortho-Bionomy: A path to self-care*, Berkeley, Ca:North Atlantic Books

Paheer, P. & Corke, A. (2018) *The Power of Good People.* Melbourne, Australia:Wild Dingo Press

Pak, C. (2017) *Transcendence in Resilient American POWs: A Narrative Analysis*, Ph.D. dissertation submitted to the Faculty of the School of Theology and Religious Studies of The Catholic University of America

Potter, B.A. (2005) *Overcoming job burnout: How to renew enthusiasm for work* (2nd ed.) Ronin Publishing

Qato, D.M., Ozenberger, K. & Olfson, M., (2018) Prevalence of Prescription Medications With Depression as a Potential Adverse Effect Among Adults in the United States, *JAMA* 319(22):2289-2298

Ramsden, E. & Adams, J. (2009) *Escaping the Laboratory: The Rodent Experiments of John B. Calhoun & Their Cultural Influence.* https://core.ac.uk/display/94997

Read, J., Agar, K., Barker-Collo, S., Davies, E. & Moskowitz, A. (2001) Assessing suicidality in adults: integrating childhood trauma as a major risk factor. *Prof Psychol Res Pr* 32:367–372

Read. J., Agar, K., Argyle, N. & Aderhold, V. (2003) Sexual and physical assault during childhood and adulthood as predictors of hallucinations, delusions and thought disorder. *Psychol Psychother Theory Res Pract* 76:1–22

Read, J., van Os, J., Morrison, A.P. & Ross, C.A. (2005) Childhood trauma, psychosis and schizophrenia: a literature review with theoretical and clinical implications. *Acta Psychiatr Scand* 112:330–350

Rich, R. (2001) *Anikó: The stranger who loved me*, Healesville, Victoria, Australia:Anina's Book Company

Rich, R. (2005) *Cancer: A personal challenge*, Healesville, Victoria, Australia:Anina's Book Company

Rich, R. (2010) *Healing Scripts* CD, http://bobswriting.com/psych/heal.html

Rich, R. (2013) *Ascending Spiral: Humanity's last chance*, Marvelous Spirit Press

Rich, R. (2015) *You too can live in contentment,* PDF file

Rich, R. (2018) *Hit and Run*, Writers Exchange E-publishing

Rogers, C.R. (1942). *Counseling and psychotherapy.* Cambridge, MA:Riverside Press

Rogers, C. R. (1951) *Client-Centered Therapy*, Boston:Houghton-Mifflin

Schober, J.P., Stensland, K.D., Breyer, B.N., Erickson, B.A., Myers, J.B., Voelzke, B.B., Elliott, S.P., Buckley, J.C. & Vanni, A.J. (2018) Effect of Urethroplasty on Anxiety and Depression, *J. Urol.* 5347(18):30116-2

Segal, J.E., Hunter, J. & Segal, Z. (1978) *Universal consequences of captivity: stress reactions among divergent populations of prisoners of war and their families,* Report NO. 75—84, Naval Health Research Center, 7 San Diego, California

Seligman, M.E.P. (1988) In J. Buie, 'Me' decades generate depression: individualism erodes commitment to others. *APA Monitor*, 19, 18

Seligman, M.E.P. (2002) *Authentic Happiness*, Random House

Seligman, M.E.P. (2007) *The Optimistic Child*, Wilmington, MA:Mariner Books

Sullivan, P.F., Neale, M.C. & Kendler, K.S. (2000) Genetic Epidemiology of Major Depression: Review and Meta-Analysis, *American Journal of Psychiatry*, 157(10):1552-1562

Terr, L.C. (1991) Childhood traumas: An outline and overview, *Am J Psychiatry*, 148:10-20

Tucker, J. B. (2005) Life Before Life: A scientific investigation of children's memories of previous lives, New York:St. Martin's Press

Tucker, J.B. (2013) *Return to Life*, Macmillan

Tyrell, M. & Elliott. R. *Major Depression Facts*, http://www.clinical-depression.co.uk/dlp/depression-information/major-depression-facts/

Whitaker, R. (2010) Anatomy of an Epidemic: Magic Bullets, Psychiatric Drugs and the rise of Mental Illness in America. New York: Broadway Books Crown Publishing Group

White, M., & Epston, D. (1989) *Literate means to therapeutic ends*, Adelaide, South Australia:Dulwich Centre Publications

About the Author

Bob Rich, Ph.D. earned his doctorate in psychology in 1972. He worked as an academic, researcher and applied scientist until "retiring" the first time at 36 years of age. Later, he returned to psychology and qualified as a Counseling Psychologist, running a private practice for over 20 years. During this time, he was on the national executive of the College of Counselling Psychologists of the Australian Psychological Society (APS), then spent three years as a Director of the APS. He was the therapist referrers sent their most difficult cases to.

Bob retired in 2013, but still does pro bono counseling over the internet. This has given him hundreds of "children" and "grandchildren" he has never met, because many of these people stay in touch for years. His major joy in life is to be of benefit to others, which is why he wrote a book that's in effect a course of therapy.

You can get to know him well at his blog, *Bobbing Around*, https://bobrich18.wordpress.com

Index

A

Adams, J., 41
Alder, C., 108
antidepressant, 6, 10, 17, 84, 104
assertive communication, 133

B

Beck, A., 39
between lives, 36–37
bipolar disorder, 36–37
Buddhism, 107, 108, 109, 110, 121
burnout
  defined, 34

C

Calhoun, J., 41–43
childhood trauma, 38–40
children's past life recalls, 111
Chopra, D., 24, 119
cocaine, 35, 45
comorbidity, 33, 139
consumer myth, 45, 46
Corke, A., 95
creativity, 11–12
Csikszentmihályi, 104, 106, 107

D

Dalai Lama, 98, 107, 120, 130, 134
depression
  as disease, 33
  major, 36
  post-partum, 34
  symptoms, 31–32
do the opposite, 5–6

Doom Healer, 123
DSM 5, 31, 33
Dysthymia, 35

E

eating
  healthy, 7–8
Elliot, R., 1
empathy, 130
Epston, D., 70
equanimity, 122–25, 135
exercise, 10

F

Flannery, T., 43
Frankl, V., 6, 18, 35, 93, 96

G

Gathercole, M., 2
genuineness, 130
Goodman, M., 66
Greenberg, G., 31, 138
grief, 9, 10
  anticipatory, 34
Guardian Angel, 47
guided imagery, 26–29
guilt, 129

H

happiness myth, 43
healthy eating, 7–8
hedonic adaptation, 44, 82, 96
heredity
  and depression, 37–38
heroin, 35

Hoopes, L., 50
hypnosis, 110

I

ICD 10, 31, 138

J

Jesus, 47, 65, 98, 109, 124
journaling, 49

K

karma, 102, 119, 120

L

Lyuobomisky, S., 96

M

Mazari, N., 95, 96
meaning, 14
    lack of, 35
meditation
    mindfulness, 22–26
methamphetamine, 35
metta, 98, 99, 100, 109, 121, 123,
    124, 130, 131, 133, 134
mindfulness meditation, 22–26
Mother Teresa, 43, 83
muscular relaxation, 19–22

N

Narrative Therapy, 70, 71, 72, 89,
    90, 92
Neeld, E.H., 34
Noble Truths, 108–9

O

Overmeyer, L., 113

P

Packer, K., 119
Paheer, P., 95
planned obsolescence, 46
population pressure, 41–43
post-partum depression, 34
Post-Traumatic Stress Disorder. *See*
    PTSD
Potter, B., 34
PTSD, 33, 88, 94, 95, 138
    defined, 32

R

Ramsden, E., 41
Ramster, P., 110
reincarnation, 109–19
    and suicide, 120
relaxation
    muscular, 19
REM sleep, 8
resilience, 50–51
Rogers, C., 130
Rowan, Y., 113

S

SAD, 34
sadnes, 33–37
Seasonal Affective Disorder. *See* SAD
secondary gains, 65–68
Seligman, M., 1, 92, 107, 134
Siddhartha, 107
sleep, 8–10
social connectedness, 12–14
Stevenson, I., 111
stress-related diseases, 41
Sutcliffe, W., 123

T

Terr, L., 39
Tucker, J., 111–12, 120
Twain, M., 108
Tyrell, M., 1

U

unconditional positive regard, 130

V

Vipassana, 108

W

Whitaker, W., 31
White, M., 70

Y

Yousafzai, M., 44

Z

Zinn, J.K., 26, 122, 125

Join us on an epic journey older than civilization itself

Dr. Pip Lipkin has lived for 12,000 years, incarnated many times as man, woman, and even as species beyond our world and senses. But he's here for a reason: to pay restitution for an ancient crime by working to save humanity from certain destruction. *Ascending Spiral* is a book that will take the reader to many different places and times, showing, ultimately, that our differences and divisions, even at their most devastating, are less important than our similarities.

Reviewers' Acclaim

"Bob Rich powerfully evokes the wounded healer archetype in *Ascending Spiral*, taking readers on Pip's painful and insightful journey through lifetimes that serve as a shining example of how to turn misery into virtue."

--Diane Wing, author, *Coven: Scrolls of the Four Winds*

"Dr. Bob Rich's *Ascending Spiral* is a true genre-buster, incorporating elements of historical fiction, literary fiction, science fiction, and even a hint of nonfiction to create an entertaining novel with an important message."

Magdalena Ball, CompulsiveReader.com

"The way of karma rings true for many people, and this book is a very well written and thoughtful explanation of its message. It is also an exciting, historically accurate series of linked stories that will hold the reader in his chair for a single sitting. Highly recommended."

Frances Burke, author of *Endless Time*

From Marvelous Spirit Press
www.MarvelousSpirit.com
"Books that maximize empowerment of mind and spirit"

CPSIA information can be obtained
at www.ICGtesting.com
Printed in the USA
BVHW040002230219
540984BV00006B/28/P